Critical thinking
A Beginner's Guide

ONEWORLD BEGINNER'S GUIDES combine an original, inventive, and engaging approach with expert analysis on subjects ranging from art and history to religion and politics, and everything in between. Innovative and affordable, books in the series are perfect for anyone curious about the way the world works and the big ideas of our time.

anarchism	dewey	mafia & organized crime
anticapitalism	dyslexia	marx
artificial intelligence	energy	medieval philosophy
the baha'i faith	engineering	NATO
the beat generation	evolution	oil
biodiversity	evolutionary psychology	the palestine–israeli conflict
bioterror & biowarfare	existentialism	paul
the brain	fair trade	philosophy of mind
the buddha	forensic science	philosophy of religion
censorship	genetics	postmodernism
christianity	global terrorism	psychology
cloning	hinduism	quantum physics
crimes against humanity	humanism	the qur'an
criminal psychology	islamic philosophy	racism
critical thinking	lacan	religion
daoism	life in the universe	the small arms trade
democracy	machiavelli	sufism

Critical thinking
A Beginner's Guide

Sharon M. Kaye

ONEWORLD

OXFORD

A Oneworld Paperback Original

Published by Oneworld Publications 2009

Copyright © Sharon M. Kaye 2009

The right of Sharon M. Kaye to be identified as the Author of
this work has been asserted by her in accordance with the
Copyright, Designs and Patents Act 1988

ISBN 978–1–85168–654–4

Typeset by Jayvee, Trivandrum, India
Cover design by Simon McFadden
Printed and bound in Great Britain by TJ International, Padstow

Oneworld Publications
185 Banbury Road
Oxford OX2 7AR
England
www.oneworld-publications.com

Mixed Sources
Product group from well-managed
forests and other controlled sources
www.fsc.org Cert no. SGS-COC-2482
© 1996 Forest Stewardship Council

Learn more about Oneworld. Join our mailing list to
find out about our latest titles and special offers at:

www.oneworld-publications.com

Contents

Preface

I will never forget my first logic class.

I am sitting in a large lecture hall at the University of Wisconsin in Madison. Outside the long, stately windows it is sunny and warm. I am surrounded by a hundred distracted students in jeans and t-shirts.

Professor Ellery Ells is up on the stage telling us that logic is the law of thought.

I am riveted, but only because I am offended. How can this man have the nerve to stand up there and tell me there are limits on what can be true? Fancying myself a poet and an artist, I resist his every word. Surely creativity is more important than clarity. Imagination is the secret to happiness and it needs no rules.

My notebook from that course is filled with rebellious floral doodles and not a few unkind sketches of Professor Ells.

But thank God for university requirements. By the time I finished the course I understood: beauty is meaningless without structure, and logic is the most powerful structure ever conceived.

So now I wake to find that I have been teaching the basic logic skills known as 'critical thinking' for over ten years.

I would like to thank my students over the years for trying to fight me the way I tried to fight Professor Ells. I would also like to thank John Carroll University for reducing my course load every semester so that I have time to write. Terry Bradley and Elizabeth Funk obtained permissions for all of the passages quoted in this book. I am grateful for their timely and effective work. Finally, I am grateful to my editor at Oneworld, Mike Harpley, for sound guidance throughout the process.

This book is dedicated to Tris and the rest of the gamesters. You all play a role in what follows.

SK

Introduction

> Insight, untested and unsupported, is an insufficient guarantee of truth.
>
> Bertrand Russell

Do you have opinions?

Of course you do.

Having opinions is how we define ourselves. It's how we forge alliances (*I like that TV show, too*) and it's how we distinguish ourselves from others (*That TV show is for idiots*).

Young children may differ from their parents in terms of aversions (*I hate green beans*) and attractions (*I love swimming*). But it takes them a while to develop opinions that contradict their parents (*This war is wrong*). Having independent opinions is the first sign of growing up.

Breaking out of the parental mould is terrifying at first, but it's also exhilarating. Teenagers often find it so exhilarating that they begin to express contrary views at every available opportunity and even to create conflict out of nothing when things get dull (*It's a free country – I can think what I want!*).

Annoying as this can be, we have to admit that having independent opinions is actually an accomplishment. Considering how much our family, our friends, the media, the government, and religious institutions try to influence us, it's amazing that anyone ever has an original thought at all.

And the fact that we have the right to think and say what we believe really is something to relish. It's one of the greatest triumphs of modern civilization. Our ancestors in the Middle

Ages simply were not permitted to disagree with authority. Brave protesters throughout history slowly changed this for us. Tragically, there are still countries around the world today without the right to free speech.

Being able to express oneself is such a great thing that sometimes people make the mistake of thinking it is the final stage of intellectual maturity – that once you've developed a unique and interesting point of view you're ready to face the world and all its challenges.

This is unfortunate. In fact, having opinions is just the beginning.

Because we live in an age of freedom, you don't *have to* defend your opinions. But don't you want to? If your opinions are more than just childish aversions and attractions, then you should be willing to take a stand for them.

Wherever you are, your point of view will give you opinions about the issues you face. But having opinions is not enough to be successful in what you do. You need to be able to transform your opinion into a *position*. The difference between an opinion and a position is that a position is supported by argument.

Anyone can make an argument. But let's face it: some arguments are better than others.

In order to make a good argument, you need to use logic. Logic is the bare bones of all human thought. Human beings are born with a natural ability to reason logically. But we are also born with the propensity to make logical errors. By uncovering and examining the logic underlying ordinary reasoning you can learn to support your opinions effectively.

Intelligent people misuse logic every day. Sometimes they do so on purpose in order to manipulate you. This happens a lot in advertising. And maybe it doesn't matter much if you are tricked into buying Coke instead of Pepsi. But manipulative logic can also be used in more important contexts, such as in a court of law.

Consider the following summation speech:

Ladies and Gentlemen of the Jury,

We have heard testimony over the past several days regarding the brutal murder of Cassandra Thomas, the owner of a corner grocery store in Gamerton. Ms Thomas was shot dead in her store on the afternoon of 10 July.

The defendant, Mr Vincent Cockley, insists he had no motive for this crime. Yet he is in debt and his ex-girlfriend attests to his psychological instability. Furthermore, although he has worked at the same company for five years, his co-workers say they feel they don't really know him.

Mr Cockley's lawyer asks us to believe that Mr Cockley is just a shy little fellow who couldn't hurt a fly. But the bottom line is this: either Mr Cockley is an upstanding citizen or he is a violent criminal. And a man who hasn't even paid his taxes for the past two years cannot be considered an upstanding citizen, shy or otherwise.

Everyone knows lying is wrong. Yet Mr Cockley admitted he lied to the police when they first questioned him concerning his whereabouts on the night of 10 July. Upon further questioning, the police learned that Mr Cockley was in the process of planning a trip to Mexico – which very nearly enabled him to escape arrest.

Mr Cockley testified that the trip was for a charity that helps needy people build homes. The charity organizer, however, testified that the construction crew is composed primarily of ex-cons. This confirms the well-known fact that criminals habitually associate with other criminals.

Mr Cockley claims that on the night of 10 July, he arrived at Ms Thomas's store just as the real killer was fleeing and that he chased the killer across town before losing him. I must remind you, however, that Mr Cockley has already lied once. How can we be expected to believe anything else he tells us?

Finally, the crime scene investigators have established that Ms Thomas's murderer wore the gloves displayed in Exhibit A. If the gloves did not fit Mr Cockley, then he would be proven innocent. But the gloves do fit him, as you witnessed with your own eyes. Therefore, Mr Cockley is guilty. And therefore, he should receive the maximum penalty.

You can probably tell at a glance that this speech is flawed. But can you find all ten errors? Can you name them and explain why they are wrong? (There is an answer key at the end of this book.)

This speech is fictional. You're not likely ever to be subjected to such a terrible line of reasoning in real life unless you're in the habit of reading advertisements for diet pills. Respectable speakers and writers try to be logical and they have editors and proofreaders who check to be sure they are.

The frightening truth is this: actual logical errors are more likely to occur in the unexamined corners of your own mind than in a public speech or in print.

For example, suppose you were not on the jury for the above case, but you were instead reading about it in a newspaper, which said the following:

. . . There has been widespread speculation that the gloves displayed in Exhibit A would never fit Mr. Cockley. During proceedings today, however, Mr. Cockley agreed to try on the gloves and they did fit . . .

After reading this paragraph, the following thought might float nonchalantly through your mind: 'Well, if the gloves didn't fit, he'd be innocent. But they did fit, so he must be guilty.'

This is bad logic. The newspaper would never print it and only the seediest lawyer would ever say it out loud. As a private thought, however, it will float through the minds of many people who read the newspaper article. While speeches and articles are subjected to careful proofreading, our thoughts often go unchecked.

Such thoughts are a menace. They lead to bad attitudes and bad decisions. They impede our ability to think clearly.

It is possible, however, to develop the mental habit of checking your own logic as well as the logic of others. This is called **critical thinking**.

People sometimes suppose the term 'critical thinker' applies to anyone who likes to criticize others. In particular, non-conformist groups and radical political organizations that criticize the government or other aspects of mainstream society often style themselves as 'critical thinkers'. They may or may not be, depending on how they go about their criticism.

True critical thinking is about using good logic. By learning the basic principles of good logic, you will be less likely to be fooled by bad logic and you will be more readily able to develop intelligent positions on important issues. This book is designed to give you all the critical thinking skills you need.

1

What is an argument?

A noble heart will always capitulate to reason.

Johann Friedrich Von Schiller

The first step toward becoming a critical thinker is to learn how to identify arguments. In everyday conversation, the term 'argument' is most often used for an angry exchange of words. People therefore typically think of an argument as an unpleasant situation to be avoided. In academic and professional circles, however, the term 'argument' has a technical meaning. An **argument** is a discussion in which reasons are advanced in favor of a proposal. Argument is the best way to support your opinions – it need not be angry or unpleasant at all.

Standard form

In order to identify and study arguments we rewrite them in standard form. **Standard form** is a schema for identifying the steps of an argument. This is the general format:

1. The first reason is . . .
2. The second reason is . . .

_____

3. Therefore, the proposal is . . .

The steps above the line are called the 'premises' while the final step below the line is called the 'conclusion'.

   An argument can contain any number of premises leading to a single conclusion. It can also contain a series of subconclusions. A **subconclusion** is a conclusion that functions as a premise for a further conclusion. For example:

1. Hybrids are the most efficient cars.
2. The most efficient cars are cheapest to drive.

---

3. So, hybrids are the cheapest to drive.
4. I should buy whatever car is cheapest to drive.

---

5. Therefore, I should buy a hybrid.

Step 3 of this standard form is a subconclusion. It is conventional to signal subconclusions by the word 'So' instead of the word 'Therefore' in order to tell the reader more is coming.

Although arguments are everywhere, they are often difficult to recognize. This is because authors almost never present their arguments in standard form. Instead they typically couch them within long expositions, leaving it to the reader to figure out exactly what the premises and conclusions are.

The following is a rare case in which author William Lane Craig not only tells you he is about to discuss an argument, but also lays out its steps for you in standard form.

PROFESSOR MACKIE AND THE *KALAM* COSMOLOGICAL ARGUMENT

[I]n this piece I should like to focus on Mackie's analysis of one particular argument, the *kalam* cosmological argument. For his discussion at this point seems to me to be superficial, and I think it can be shown that he has failed to provide any compelling or even intuitively appealing objection against the argument.

The *kalam* argument . . . may be schematized:

1. Whatever begins to exist has a cause of its existence.
2. The universe began to exist.
   . . . .
3. Therefore, the universe has a cause of its existence.

W. L. Craig, 'Professor Mackie and the *kalam* cosmological argument', *Religious Studies* 20 (1985), pp. 367–8

Craig's standard form presentation of the *kalam* argument sets him up for a well-organized discussion of the issue. His proposal is that the universe has a cause of its existence. His opponent, Mackie, maintains the opposite – that the universe could be uncaused. Faced with Craig's argument, Mackie will have to explain which of Craig's premises he finds objectionable.

Anticipating Mackie will focus his objection against premise two, Craig proceeds to add two subarguments to support this premise, ending up with an eleven-step argument:

1. Whatever begins to exist has a cause of its existence.
2. The universe began to exist.
    2.1 Argument based on the impossibility of an actual infinite:
        2.11 An actual infinite cannot exist.
        2.12 An infinite temporal regress of events is an actual infinite.
        2.13 Therefore, an infinite temporal regress of events cannot exist.
    2.2 Argument based on the impossibility of the formation of an actual infinite by successive addition:
        2.21 A collection formed by successive addition cannot be actually infinite.
        2.22 The temporal series of past events is a collection formed by successive addition.
        2.23 Therefore, the temporal series of past events cannot be actually infinite.
3. Therefore, the universe has a cause of its existence.

Needless to say, there are a lot of technical concepts in these subarguments, which Craig will need to define and explain. We don't need to get into any of these details, however, to see that Craig's argument constitutes a formidable challenge to Mackie.

A reader who was already familiar with the *kalam* argument would no doubt welcome Craig's schematic presentation since it captures the issue in such a clear and logical way. Would it be better if everyone always wrote schematically like Craig? Imagine a world in which politicians laid out their arguments in standard form! Perhaps we would have an easier time figuring out where they actually stand, but we would also never get a sense of their personalities, and we might just fall asleep before they'd finished. It's probably just as well that most authors don't schematize their arguments for us. This leaves us, the readers, with something to figure out. We have to read actively, thereby gaining the opportunity to interpret the author in our own way.

Consider the following passage from Napoleon Hill's classic motivational book of the 1930s, *Think and Grow Rich*. Selling more than thirty million copies worldwide, this book is still today ranked in the top ten on the *Business Week* Best-seller List. It is completely different from the Craig passage in both style and content, yet it contains an argument just the same.

THE MYSTERY OF SEX TRANSMUTATION

The emotion of sex brings into being a state of mind.

Because of ignorance on the subject, this state of mind is generally associated with the physical, and because of improper influences, to which most people have been subjected in acquiring knowledge of sex, things essentially physical have highly biased the mind.

The emotion of sex has back of it the possibility of three constructive potentialities. They are:

1. The perpetuation of mankind.
2. The maintenance of health (as a therapeutic agency, it has no equal).
3. The transformation of mediocrity into genius through transmutation.

THE MYSTERY OF SEX TRANSMUTATION (*cont.*)

Sex transmutation is simple and easily explained. It means the switching of the mind from thoughts of physical expression to thoughts of some other nature.

Sex desire is the most powerful of human desires. When driven by this desire, men develop keenness of imagination, courage, will-power, persistence, and creative ability unknown to them at other times. So strong and impelling is the desire for sexual contact that men freely run the risk of life and reputation to indulge it. When harnessed, and redirected along other lines, this motivating force maintains all of its attributes of keenness of imagination, courage, etc., which may be used as powerful creative forces in literature, art, or in any other profession or calling, including, of course, the accumulation of riches.

The transmutation of sex energy calls for the exercise of will-power, to be sure, but the reward is worth the effort. The desire for sexual expression is inborn and natural. The desire cannot, and should not be submerged or eliminated. But it should be given an outlet through forms of expression which enrich the body, mind, and spirit of man. If not given this form of outlet, through transmutation, it will seek outlets through purely physical channels.

A river may be dammed, and its water controlled for a time, but eventually, it will force an outlet. The same is true of the emotion of sex. It may be submerged and controlled for a time, but its very nature causes it to be ever seeking means of expression. If it is not transmuted into some creative effort it will find a less worthy outlet.

N. Hill, *Think and Grow Rich* (New York: Fawcett Books, 1937, 1960), pp. 155–6

Although Hill's argument is somewhat rambling and repetitive, it is also colorful and interesting. What exactly is his proposal and what are the reasons he is advancing in favor of it?

In answering this question, the first thing to note is that the three numbered steps appearing in the third paragraph *do not* constitute an argument. They constitute a list. A list is nothing more than a set of items that fit a given description. An argument, in contrast, contains a proposal along with reasons that support it. Because there is no relationship of support among the items in Hill's numbered steps, we know it is a list rather than an argument.

When looking for an argument, the best thing to do is start by asking yourself: what is this author trying to prove? This is to say, what is his or her main conclusion? Answering this question will involve some interpretation. One reader may legitimately come to a slightly different answer than another reader. This doesn't mean anything goes – for example, Hill certainly is not making a proposal about rivers. His point about rivers provides an illustration for his proposal; to think it is the proposal itself would be a misunderstanding.

A definite proposal can be found in the second paragraph from the end when Hill writes: 'The desire for sexual expression . . . should be given an outlet . . . through transmutation.' Just as a river needs an outlet, so also does sexual desire, in Hill's view. Everything he says in the passage is designed to support this proposal either directly or indirectly. 'Sexual transmutation' is Hill's name for giving sexual desire a non-physical outlet in a profession or other creative calling. Hill is clearly proposing sexual transmutation.

A proposal, however, is not by itself an argument. In order to create an argument, an author needs to advance reasons in favor of his proposal. What are Hill's reasons for proposing sexual transmutation?

Hill devotes the longest paragraph of the passage to the claim that sexual desire is the most powerful human desire. Suppose we cast this claim as the first premise in his argument. Then we have the beginnings of a standard form:

1. Sexual desire is the most powerful human desire.
2. _____
3. Therefore, sexual desire should be given an outlet through transmutation.

Setting aside Hill's passage for a moment, we should now ask ourselves the question, what would it take to connect step 1 with step 3? What is the logical bridge?

What we are looking for here is something like the law of transitivity in mathematics, which is extremely important in formulating a good argument. The word 'transitive,' which comes from the Latin word for 'going across', means that a relationship holds between the members of a sequence such that the middle member makes a bridge from the first member to the last. The following is the simplest example of transitivity:

1. X is Y.
2. Y is Z.
_____
3. Therefore, X is Z.

The variable 'Y' is the bridge between 'X' and 'Z.' If X is Y and Y is Z, then X must be Z.

We can create transitive bridges with verbs other than 'is'. For example, if Jake eats bacon, and bacon contains sodium, then Jake eats sodium. But not all linking sequences are transitive. Just because Gary loves Mary and Mary loves Harry doesn't mean that Gary loves Harry. As you practice reading passages for arguments, you will learn to distinguish those sequences that are transitive from those that are not.

The logic is transitive in the case at hand. We can only conclude that sexual desire should be given an outlet through transmutation if we know both that sexual desire is the most powerful human desire and that the most powerful human desire should be given an outlet through transmutation. We can therefore fill in the standard form as follows:

1. Sexual desire is the most powerful human desire.
2. The most powerful human desire should be given an outlet through transmutation.

---

3. Therefore, sexual desire should be given an outlet through transmutation.

This is a transitive sequence of reasoning.

Sure enough, if we go back now to look at the passage, we see that, although Hill never states premise 2 explicitly, he is concerned to establish this step. He tells us that, if a powerful desire does not have an outlet, then it will eventually force itself out in less worthy expressions and that if it does have an outlet, then it will produce great things. In other words, Hill is presenting two subarguments for premise 2 much the way Craig did in his passage. So, we could further expand our schema as follows:

1. Sexual desire is the most powerful human desire.
2. The most powerful human desire should be given an outlet through transmutation.
   2.1 If it isn't given an outlet, then it will force itself in less worthy ways.
   2.2 If it is given an outlet, then it will produce great things.

---

3. Therefore, sexual desire should be given an outlet through transmutation.

We can now see why Hill thinks we should accept premise 2.

As it stands, however, this standard form gives us no reason for accepting step 2.1 or step 2.2. Hill provides the needed support for these steps through his comparison to the river. We can elaborate this comparison beyond what he actually says in order to fill out the two subarguments.

1. Sexual desire is the most powerful human desire.
2. The most powerful human desire should be given an outlet through transmutation.
   2.1 If it isn't given an outlet, then it will force itself in less worthy ways.
      2.11 If a river isn't given an outlet, it bursts through the dam.
      2.12 If a river bursts through the dam, then it causes damage.
      2.13 Therefore, if a river isn't given an outlet, then it causes damage.
   2.2 If it is given an outlet, then it will produce great things.
      2.21 If a river is given an outlet, then its energy can be harnessed.
      2.22 If a river's energy can be harnessed, then it can generate electricity for many people to use.
      2.23 Therefore, if a river is given an outlet, then it can generate electricity for many people to use.

   _____

3. Therefore, sexual desire should be given an outlet through transmutation.

Notice the transitive structure of the two subarguments. They can be taken to provide support for premise 2 of the main argument provided one's strongest desire is just like a river, as Hill claims.

Now we have a full account of Hill's argument. We know exactly what his proposal is and we understand the reasons he advances in favor of it. It took a little bit of work! We had to eliminate some elements of the passage that weren't relevant and supply other elements that were missing. Hill could have saved us a lot of trouble by presenting his argument schematically in the first place, as did Craig. But would Hill have sold thirty million copies of his book if it were full of standard form arguments? Probably not! First of all, it wouldn't be as much fun to read that way. Second, and more importantly, it would make him too vulnerable to criticism. In fact, the big pay-off for wrestling an argument into standard form is that it puts the reader in a strong position to evaluate it.

We now know Hill's argument crucially hinges on the claim that sexual desire should be given an outlet through transmutation because it is just like a river. How convincing is this claim? According to the analogy, allowing sexual desire to be expressed physically would be equivalent to allowing a river to flow naturally; meanwhile, transmuting sexual desire into a profession or other creative calling would be equivalent to damming the river and diverting its flow to generate electricity for many people to use. Hill thinks it's obvious that generating electricity is better than letting the river flow naturally. But there is plenty of room here to disagree.

For example, some environmentalists insist that interrupting the natural flow of a river is deeply and irreparably harmful to the surrounding wildlife over time. Likewise, a critic of Hill might insist that transmuting sexual desire into a profession or other creative calling is deeply and irreparably harmful to the body over time. Recall that, in his third paragraph, Hill himself states that sex 'has no equal' as a 'therapeutic agency' for 'the maintenance of health'. How are we to square this claim with his claim that we should transmute it? While it was tempting to be swept along with Hill's proposal on first read, a closer analysis reveals that it not only raises a number of important questions but also seems downright self-contradictory.

This is what critical thinkers do. To put it bluntly, we are killjoys. We hunt down breezy, fun-loving sailboats in order to snatch the wind right out of their sails. Why would anyone want to learn such a skill?

Breezy sailboats aren't fun for long if they head off into a storm because they weren't paying attention to where they were going. In the end, we are all better off if we confront the truth. Standard form evaluation enables us to confront the truth.

But does standard form really work for evaluating any argument?

Yes, it really does. (As a matter of fact, I plucked the Hill book at random from my husband's bookshelf!) And if it seems like a bit of a mystery exactly how we figured out how to wrestle Hill's argument into standard form, that's only because we're just at the beginning. By the end of this book, you'll be able to do it too.

Induction versus deduction

When you begin hunting for arguments, the first thing you will notice is that there are two fundamentally different types.

In the empirical sciences, such as physics, biology, psychology, and sociology, you will most often run into the type of argument known as induction. An **inductive argument** is a line of reasoning that produces only a probable conclusion. This is to say that, even if all the premises of the argument are true, the conclusion may still be false.

The familiar science of weather forecasting uses inductive logic to predict future weather patterns based on what has occurred in the past. Without any sophisticated equipment or formulas, we have all made our own weather forecasts, reasoning in the following way:

1. It snowed in New York City last December.
2. It snowed in New York City two Decembers ago.
3. It snowed in New York City three Decembers ago.
4. etc.

_____

5. Therefore, it will snow in New York City this December.

This is an inductive argument.

The distinctive feature of inductive arguments is that the truth of the premises does not guarantee the truth of the conclusion. We might be 100 percent certain that it has snowed in December for the past one hundred Decembers. Nevertheless, we still cannot be 100 percent certain that this December will be the same. To emphasize this, weather forecasters often quantify their conclusions in statistical terms: 'We estimate a 95 percent chance of snow sometime this month.'

A **deductive argument**, in contrast, is a line of reasoning in which the truth of the premises guarantees the truth of the conclusion. This is to say that, if all the premises in the argument are true, then the conclusion has to be true. Inductive arguments can often be converted into deductive arguments and vice versa. The following is a deductive version of our inductive argument above.

1. If it has snowed in New York City every December for the past one hundred years, then it will snow there this December.
2. It has snowed in New York City every December for the past one hundred years.

---

3. Therefore, it will snow there this December.

This argument forces the author to take a stand on the reliability of past weather patterns. Ignoring statistical estimates, it states a general principle (in premise 1) and then proceeds to confirm that principle (in premise 2), yielding an inescapable conclusion.

So, does this mean the deductive argument definitely proves that it will snow in New York City this December while the inductive argument doesn't?

No. The two arguments are equally uncertain. While the inductive argument holds uncertainty in its conclusion, the deductive argument holds the same uncertainty in its first premise. The principle stated in the first premise is 'If it has snowed in New York City every December for the past one hundred years, then it will snow there this December'. This is highly disputable: something significant may have changed this year to make the conditions different. Deduction tells us that, *if* the premises are true, then the conclusion has to be true, but it cannot guarantee that the premises are in fact true.

So, given that the two arguments are equally uncertain, what's the difference? Is there a reason for using one method of reasoning as opposed to the other?

We typically use induction when we have empirical data to plug into the premises. Many of the issues we face, however, defy empirical measurement. In that case, we use deduction. Consider the following deductive argument about American and British law:

1. If abortion is always wrong, then Roe v. Wade and the Abortion Act should be repealed.
2. Abortion is always wrong.

---

3. Therefore, Roe v. Wade and the Abortion Act should be repealed.

This argument states a principle in the first premise and then confirms it in the second premise. If you agree to these two premises, then there is no escaping the conclusion. Nevertheless, you don't have to agree to the premises.

Suppose someone wanted to avoid uncertainty in the premises by making a case against abortion inductively:

1. The first abortion was wrong.
2. The second abortion was wrong.
3. The third abortion was wrong.
4. etc.

---

5. Therefore, all abortions are wrong.

This effort is absurd. Even if you could actually find some way to identify a proper sample of abortions, there is no way to test them for wrongness. Wrongness is a matter of judgment that is not empirically measurable.

Although science cannot settle legal issues for us, decisions need to be made, and so people need to take their stands. Deduction forces people to formulate their opinions into clear principles that can be evaluated. Someone who disagreed with the deductive argument about abortion could generate an example of an abortion that did not seem wrong. This would cast doubt on premise 2 ('Abortion is always wrong'), thereby destroying the inference to the conclusion.

Remember: in a deductive argument, if the premises are true, then the conclusion has to be true. But if the premises aren't true, then all bets are off. This is why, when evaluating deductive arguments, we challenge the premises rather than the conclusion. The conclusion *follows from* the premises. So, if there is a problem with the conclusion, that problem will have its source in one or more of the premises. Evaluating a deductive argument means attacking the premise you find most controversial.

Although inductive arguments are typically used in connection with scientific issues, one type of inductive argument appears regularly in both scientific and non-scientific issues, namely, argument by analogy. An **argument by analogy** is an argument that draws a conclusion about one thing based on its likeness to another thing.

We have already witnessed argument by analogy at work in the Hill passage when he compares sexual desire to a river. It is necessary to see why arguments by analogy are a form of induction in order to evaluate them effectively.

Suppose someone says the following:

> Lindy and Laurie are twin sisters. I mean they are just alike! And Lindy is definitely married. So, I imagine Laurie is too.

How would this argument be represented in standard form? Here is a first try:

1. Lindy is like Laurie.
2. Lindy is married.

---

3. Therefore, Laurie is married.

This is not a deductive argument. We can tell because the premises could both be true while the conclusion is false. Just because two people are alike doesn't mean they're alike in every way! In fact, it's impossible for any two people to be alike in every way – twins or not. So, even though the premises are both certain, there is uncertainty in the conclusion. Recall from our discussion, above, that uncertainty in the conclusion is the mark of inductive, not deductive, arguments.

Although the argument doesn't look like our inductive argument about snow in New York City on the surface, a deeper analysis reveals the same structure. After all, why would someone say Lindy and Laurie are 'just alike' unless they had a whole list of qualities in mind adding up in the following way:

1. Lindy and Laurie are both in their forties.
2. Lindy and Laurie are both religious.
3. Lindy and Laurie both have children.
4. etc.

---

5. Therefore, Lindy and Laurie are both married.

The structure of this argument is similar to the inductive version of the snow argument because it presents a number of known cases as evidence for how an unknown case must be.

Arguments by analogy are dangerous because they are highly persuasive. The list of similarities between Lindy and Laurie paints a picture in our minds of a certain kind of person that seems to fit with marriage. Premise 3 especially seems to seal the deal—surely if they both have children they both must be married.

Not necessarily! There are of course plenty of instances of non-married mothers. The truth is that we have no basis for eliminating this possibility. So, what is the critical thinker to do with such an argument?

As in the case of the snow argument, it may help to convert it into deductive form so that we can clearly see what principles are at stake. This is basically what we did when we examined Hill's analogy between sexual desire and a river. That analogy could be captured in the following standard form:

1. A river is related to a dam in the same way sexual desire is related to transmutation.
2. A river should be given a controlled outlet through a dam in order to harness its energy.

---

3. Therefore, sexual desire should be given a controlled outlet through transmutation in order to harness its energy.

This format is deductive because, if the premises are true, the conclusion has to be true. It is also useful because it reveals the principle the author is relying on and gives us a clear basis for evaluation. Recall that we said someone might object to premise 2 because dams are damaging to the environment.

We could do the same thing for the argument about the sisters:

1. Lindy is related to Mike in the same way that Laurie is related to Russ.
2. Lindy is married to Mike.

---

3. Therefore, Laurie is married to Russ.

This argument, like the one immediately above it, is deductive. Its conclusion has to be true if its premises are true. But are the premises true? It is now evident that everything hinges on premise 1. Are the members of the first pair really related to each other in the same way as the members of the second pair? It will be hard to answer this question if we don't know whether or not Laurie is married. Conversely, if we did know for certain that the two pairs were related in the same way, then why would there be any question about whether or not Laurie is married?

The pattern for the deductive reconstruction of arguments by analogy can be represented symbolically as follows:

1. $a : b :: c : d$ ('a is to b just as c is to d')
2. $a\text{--}P\text{--}b$ ('a is related to b through P')

---

3. $c\text{--}P\text{--}d$ ('Therefore, c is related to d through P')

The lower-case letters a, b, c, and d represent the individuals being compared, while the upper case letter P represents the property they allegedly have in common.

Once you reconstruct an analogy in deductive form you take all of the persuasive oomph out of it. In the case at hand, the reconstruction reveals how poorly the alleged evidence supports the conclusion. We shouldn't now be any more convinced that Laurie is married than we were before we were told that she is 'just like Lindy'.

So the killjoys strike again! As critical thinkers, we need not apologize for deflating an analogy as long as we shed light on the issue – which we did in both of the arguments we examined. In the case of the sexual desire analogy, we revealed that Hill was ignoring the problems damming a river may cause – problems that may have correlates in the case of sexual transmutation. In the case of the sisters, we learned that we would have to know something about the men Lindy and Laurie are related to in order to claim they were both married. And if we knew enough about those relationships, then we wouldn't need to know anything about the other ways the two women are alike. What we learned, in other words, is that being sisters really has no bearing on marital status. So, in both cases, we nailed some bad logic. Worth it? Absolutely.

Validity and soundness

Because arguments stem from opinion it may at first seem inappropriate to try to evaluate them. But we make good judgments about opinions all the time, for example, when we vote for a political candidate or hire a plumber. Making good judgments is a matter of applying reliable criteria.

There are two criteria for evaluating deductive arguments.

The first is 'validity'. In everyday conversation people use the term 'valid' to mean they agree. People often say 'That's a valid point'. This is an informal use of the term that you will need to set aside when doing logic.

In logic, the term 'valid' has a technical meaning concerning the structure of the argument. An argument is **valid** when the premises imply the conclusion such that, if the premises are true, the conclusion has to be true.

We actually already met validity in the last section when we introduced the notion of deduction. A valid argument is nothing other than a properly formed deductive argument. For example, the following argument is valid:

1. Money is more valuable than good looks.
2. Freedom is more valuable than money.

---

3. Therefore, freedom is more valuable than good looks.

If the premises are true, then the conclusion has to be true. We can see this in a flash by symbolizing the argument as follows:

1. M > G
2. F > M
   _____

3. F > G

Any numbers you plug into this equation will come out correct. Let M = 2, G = 1, and F = 3. Given the premises, the conclusion is inescapable. So, arguments with this structure are properly formed deductive arguments.

Validity is a useful criterion for judging arguments because someone might try to make a deductive argument but fail to form it properly, in which case we call it 'invalid'. For example, the following is an invalid argument:

1. Courage is more important than honesty.
2. Kindness is more important than honesty.
   _____

3. Therefore, courage and kindness are equally important.

In this argument, the premises do not imply the conclusion. A quick glance at the symbolization proves it.

1. C > H
2. K > H
   _____

3. C = K

Let C = 2, H = 1, and K = 3. In this case, the premises are true but the conclusion is false. Granted, if we instead let C = 2 and K = 2, then we would have true premises with a true conclusion. But the point is that the premises give us no guarantee that C and K are both equal to the same number. Therefore, there is no guarantee they are equal to each other. We are left with uncertainty in the conclusion – which is not permitted in deduction.

Notice that validity concerns only the structure of the argument, not the content. When you check to see whether a deductive argument is properly formed, it makes absolutely no difference whether or not you agree with it. Consider the following example:

1. Oscar is a party animal.
2. Party animals never stay home alone on Saturday night.

---

3. Therefore, Oscar never stays home alone on Saturday night.

This is a valid argument because, *if* the premises are true, then the conclusion has to be true.

Suppose you happen to know, however, that the conclusion is false: in fact, Oscar does sometimes stay home alone on Saturday night. This does not mean that the argument is invalid! On the contrary. It means that there must be a problem in one of the premises – because the conclusion follows from them. If Oscar sometimes stays home alone on Saturday night then either: (1) Oscar is not a party animal; or (2) it just isn't true that party animals never stay home alone on Saturday night. You get to decide which premise to challenge. Perhaps you will challenge them both.

Validity is not a matter of your agreement or disagreement; it is a matter of the relationship between the premises and the conclusion. It may strike you as strange to call an argument 'valid' if you disagree with it. But we need a word for arguments that are structured correctly so that we can distinguish them from arguments that are structured incorrectly. Consider the following argument:

1. Oscar is a party animal.
2. Felix is Oscar's roommate.

---

3. Therefore, Felix is a party animal.

This is an invalid argument because the premises do not imply the conclusion. Even if you happen to agree with each of the steps, the steps do not add up the way they should. It is entirely possible that Felix is the exact opposite of Oscar even though they happen to be rooming together.

Validity is an objective criterion that does not depend on opinion. Either the premises imply the conclusion or they do not. If they do not, then you need to start over. If they do, then you are ready to move on to the second criterion.

The second criterion for evaluating deductive arguments is 'soundness'. Like the word 'valid,' the word 'sound' is used in an informal way in everyday conversation. For example, if you say 'Earl has sound judgment', you're basically saying you agree with the way Earl thinks. In logic, however, 'soundness' has a technical meaning. An argument is **sound** when (1) it is valid and (2) its premises are true.

Logicians deliberately made validity part of the definition of soundness to force you to check for correct structure in an argument *before* examining its content. They knew this would be hard for you to do! When people first look at an argument, their natural instinct is to evaluate the content first. This is a mistake because if the structure is incorrect, you will have to start over anyway. We can use the following analogy to establish this point.

Suppose you are a house inspector sent to evaluate an old, abandoned house. As you approach, you can see through the window that it is full of strange and interesting furniture. So you dash inside to have a look. Unfortunately, you forgot to check the structure of the house first. The floor gives way and you fall to your death on the cement in the basement.

This analogy is a warning: always look at structure before you look at content even though you will be tempted to look at content first!

Politicians exploit the human temptation to put content before structure. A politician might make the following argument:

1. War is terrible.
2. Education is good.

3. People need to work together.
   _____

4. Therefore, you should vote for me!

If you are focused on the content of this argument you might be impressed. Who could disagree? The problem, however, is that the argument does not add up. The premises do not imply the conclusion. There is no necessary connection between the final proposal and the reasons advanced in favor of it.

When you encounter an argument like this, do not proceed! Throw it away and start over. When (and only when) you have established that an argument is valid, you can proceed to examine its content.

While validity is an objective judgment, soundness is a subjective judgment. We can see this by returning to our first example of deductive validity:

1. Money is more valuable than good looks.
2. Freedom is more valuable than money.
   _____

3. Therefore, freedom is more valuable than good looks.

We have already established that the premises imply the conclusion. So it is valid. But are the premises true? There will be different views here and no way to establish with certainty which one is correct. Some people will say the argument is sound while others say it isn't. That's fine. We don't expect people to agree about soundness the way we expect them to agree about validity.

Remember: uncertainty in the premises is the mark of deductive arguments. Some deductive arguments may seem quite certain. For example, a historian might argue:

1. Cleopatra was a woman.
2. Cleopatra was a ruler of Egypt.
   _____

3. Therefore, a woman was the ruler of Egypt.

Few people would dispute this argument. It is valid, and perhaps its premises have never been doubted. Nevertheless, we still consider it a matter of opinion to call it sound in so far as it is *possible* for someone to disagree with the premises.

We can imagine, for instance, someone uncovering some sort of evidence suggesting that Cleopatra was actually a man in drag. It doesn't matter how far-out this challenge to premise 1 might be. The point is that it is not impossible. People have a right to their opinions, no matter how crazy.

Of course, there is an objective answer to the question of whether Cleopatra was a woman or a man. But there is no final, definitive way to *prove* the answer. And if you think about it, you'll see that the same goes for every factual claim, no matter how obvious. For example, there is no way to prove that you are reading this book right now because it's possible that you are actually in a mental hospital dreaming the whole thing! So, soundness is always considered a subjective judgment. When you call an argument 'sound' you are saying that *you believe* the content to be true.

Validity, on the other hand, is not a subjective judgment because, when the premises of an argument imply its conclusion, it is *not possible* for the premises to be true while the conclusion is false. Consider the symbolic representation of our Cleopatra argument:

1. $C = W$
2. $C = R$

---

3. $W = R$

No one can escape this inference. If you try to deny it, you're not crazy, you're simply wrong. Denying this inference would be like denying that $2 + 2 = 4$. If a child were to assert that $2 + 2 = 5$, we would say that he better look again, not that he has a right to his opinion.

Soundness is the highest praise you can give an argument because it means that the argument is valid and that it has true premises in your view.

You may be wondering why the definition of soundness doesn't say that the conclusion should be true. The answer is that it doesn't need to. Think about it: Validity + True Premises = True Conclusion. The two components of the definition of soundness imply the truth of the conclusion.

We have already seen that a valid argument can be unsound. But can a sound argument be invalid?

Since the definition of soundness presupposes validity, the answer is a resounding 'no'. Nevertheless, sometimes people are fooled by an argument like the following:

1. An apple is a fruit.
2. A banana is a fruit.

---

3. Therefore, a pear is a fruit.

The premises do not imply the conclusion, so we know it is not valid. Is it sound? It *can't* be sound – because it isn't valid.

But the premises and the conclusion are true!

So what? It's just a list. We can't call a list of true statements a sound argument. Soundness is our highest praise for arguments. We reserve it for arguments we regard as perfect. An argument whose premises do not imply its conclusion is far from perfect. If you need a word to describe arguments like this one about fruit, you can say it 'contains true statements' or something to that effect. But do not call it sound!

So, critical thinkers have two criteria for evaluating arguments, one objective (validity) and one subjective (soundness). Just because soundness is subjective does not mean anything goes. Some subjective judgments are more reasonable than others. There are a lot of things critical thinkers can do to be sure their judgments are maximally reasonable. We will learn more about them in subsequent chapters.

Exercises

The following passages contain arguments by analogy. Reconstruct them in valid (deductive) standard form using the pattern we learned:

1. a : b :: c : d   ('a is to b just as c is to d')
2. a–P–b   ('a is related to b through P')

---

3. c–P–d   ('Therefore, c is related to d through P')

Here are five steps to follow for success:

(1) Draw a blank, three-step standard form:
   1.
   2.

---

   3. Therefore,
(2) Fill in the conclusion. This is the main thing the author is trying to prove to you.
   1.
   2.

---

   3. Therefore, c is related to d through P.
(3) Copy c and d to their proper place in premise 1, and P to its proper place in premise 2.
   1. ——————————— just as c is to d.
   2. P

---

   3. Therefore, c is related to d through P.
(4) Fill in a and b. These are the things c and d are being compared to.

1. a is to b just as c is to d.
2. a is related to b through P.

---

3. Therefore, c is related to d through P.

(5) Bear in mind that you will need to reword the generic phrase 'is related to' in accordance with the language of the passage. Also, feel free to translate the author's ideas into your own words. Since argument reconstruction requires interpretation, there will be more than one way to do it. Scribble possibilities on scrap paper. You can't expect to solve a puzzle on the first try! When you think you have an accurate reconstruction, check it against the key at the back of this book.

Cultural studies

Find two analogies.

> Prejudice is one of the inescapable consequences of living in a racist society. Cultural racism – the cultural images and messages that affirm the assumed superiority of Whites and the assumed inferiority of people of color – is like smog in the air. Sometimes it is so thick it is visible, other times it is less apparent, but always, day in and day out, we are breathing it in. None of us would introduce ourselves as smog-breathers (and most of us don't want to be described as prejudiced), but if we live in a smoggy place, how can we avoid breathing the air? If we live in an environment in which we are bombarded with stereotypical images in the media, are frequently exposed to the ethnic jokes of friends and family members, and are rarely informed of the accomplishments of oppressed groups, we will develop the negative categorizations of those groups that form the basis of prejudice.
>
> People of color as well as Whites develop these categorizations. Even a member of the stereotyped group may internalize

the stereotypical categories about his or her own group to some degree. In fact, this process happens so frequently that it has a name, internalized oppression.

I sometimes visualize the ongoing cycle of racism as a moving walkway at the airport. Active racist behavior is equivalent to walking fast on the conveyor belt. The person engaged in active racist behavior has identified with the ideology of White supremacy and is moving with it. Passive racist behavior is equivalent to standing still on the walkway. No overt effort is being made, but the conveyor belt moves the bystanders along to the same destination as those who are actively walking. Some of the bystanders may feel the motion of the conveyor belt, see the active racists ahead of them, and choose to turn around, unwilling to go to the same destination as the White supremacists. But unless they are walking actively in the opposite direction at a speed faster than the conveyor belt – unless they are actively anti-racist – they will find themselves carried along with the others.

> Beverly Daniel Tatum, 'Defining Racism: Can We Talk?'
> in *Readings for Diversity and Social Justice*,
> ed. M. Adams et al., (Routledge, 2000), pp. 79–81.

Aesthetics

A work's artistic success can depend upon the audience's agreement with its ethical orientation, and failure to meet this condition can impede the response required for the work's artistic success.

This, I suggest, is the right way to draw an analogy between artworks and friends. Recall that on my reading, we must agree with a person's ethos in order to appreciate some of the qualities that would make her a friend. That is, agreement in ethos is a condition of enjoyment of other potential friend-making qualities. Now consider the following case. A keen sense of adventure is one quality that might make a person a good friend. This aspect of a person's personality would be analogous to an artistically valuable feature of a work; just as this feature of the work is part of what makes the work good qua work of art, so the keen sense of adventure is part of what might make the person valuable as a friend. But now imagine that the person's keen sense of adventure manifests itself only in the following manner: this person likes to go to gay bars and invite young men to come home with him, but upon leaving the bar he assaults the young men and leaves them wounded in a nearby alley. (Although repugnant, this is surely a kind of adventure in that it involves violence, danger, and risk.) If we find this kind of activity ethically reprehensible, then it would be difficult or even impossible to appreciate the keen sense of adventure that would otherwise have made the person a good candidate for friendship. In this case the friend-making quality depends upon a response – approval of gay bashing – that we have good reason not to adopt on ethical grounds. Or to put this another way, refusal to comply with the person's ethical orientation renders inaccessible the friend-making quality that depends upon it.

The case is analogous, Hume suggests, with some works of art. It can happen that appropriate engagement with an artwork requires adopting an ethically defective attitude or perspective. This is an ethical flaw in the work and renders inaccessible those features that depend upon it. In the case where those features are artistically significant, then the work's call for an ethically defective response will impede the work's artistic success in that regard.

A.W. Eaton, 'Where Ethics and Aesthetics Meet: Titian's Rape of Europa,' *Hypatia* (Fall, 2003), Vol. 18, Issue 4, pp. 175–6

Literature

In 'Chiefly About War Matters,' narrational concerns invite questions about the politics of Hawthorne's encounter with Lincoln. 'Chiefly About War Matters' artfully damns Lincoln where it appears at first to praise him. Although many nineteenth-century readers thought the article flattering, Hawthorne's description of the 'Chief' is laced with contempt, and nowhere more artfully than in the ostensibly editorial notes to the piece. In perpetrating this literary trickery Hawthorne adopts an ironic technique suggestive of *Gulliver's Travels*. Hawthorne's narrative artistry in 'Chiefly About War Matters' specifically calls to mind Gulliver's 'publisher' – Gulliver himself posing as publisher, or else a fictive publisher contrived by Swift – who feigns authorship and censorship of his ancient and intimate friend and cousin, Gulliver, to evoke a sympathetic reaction to the narrative. Indeed, Swift added Gulliver's letter to his 'Cousin Sympson' to the 1735 Dublin edition, yet predated it April 2, 1727, to give the appearance that it had graced the book's first edition. . . .

Hawthorne, in emulating Swift's use of the editor/author letters between Gulliver, and Gulliver's 'publisher', Sympson, derives a successful pattern for his own ironic reading of Lincoln via the self-appended, though unclaimed, footnotes to his own article. Like Swift, whose political agenda is complex, Hawthorne also has a political cause advanced by this instance of narrative artistry. Although Swift's ironic treatment was somewhat more profound than simply an address to the political foibles of eighteenth-century England, his implementation of the publisher's letter and of Gulliver's remarks serves as a literary precedent for Hawthorne's use of his own footnotes to propagate a political satire of Lincoln.

I propose that Hawthorne – despite the moments of praise that define, for some readers, a respect for the nation's chief executive – uses Swiftian satirical technique to characterize Lincoln as a backwoods humorist fit only for politics. Hawthorne thereby engages in a political campaign that he declines to acknowledge openly.

Grace E. Smith, '"Chiefly About War Matters":
Hawthorne's Swift Judgment of Lincoln', *The American
Transcendental Quarterly* (June, 2001), pp. 150–1

2
Categorical syllogisms

> It is the mark of an educated mind to be able to entertain a
> thought without accepting it.
>
> Aristotle

The Ancient Greek philosopher Aristotle was the first great
logician of Western civilization. He discovered the three-step
transitive argument and called it a **syllogism**. Recall that a
three-step transitive argument looks like this:

1. X is Y.
2. Y is Z.

3. Therefore, X is Z.

Plugging in various different kinds of content for X, Y, and Z,
Aristotle realized that there are many different ways to construct
a syllogism – and only some of them are valid. He and his successors presented an account of the different types of three-step
transitive arguments. This account is known as 'the theory of the
categorical syllogism'. It is important for critical thinkers to be
familiar with this account, both because it has been used as a
model for argumentation throughout history and because it can
still help us organize our own thoughts in valid standard form.

Categorical statements

A **categorical statement** is a statement that asserts a relationship between two categories. For example, the statement 'A

cockroach is an insect' is a categorical statement because it asserts that every member of the category 'cockroach' is also a member of the category 'insect'. The formula 'X is Y' represents a categorical statement. Categorical syllogisms are composed of categorical statements.

Every categorical statement has two parts: a subject and a predicate. The **subject** is the term about which something is affirmed or denied. The **predicate** is the phrase that affirms or denies something about the subject. In the statement 'Insects are good pets', the term 'insects' is the subject and the phrase 'are good pets' is the predicate.

The goal of every categorical syllogism is to deduce a categorical statement. So, the third step or conclusion of the argument will be a statement with a subject and a predicate as follows:

1.
2.
_____

3. Therefore, subject–predicate.

Knowing that transitivity aims to connect the first member of a sequence with its last member through a bridge, we may fill in the first two steps as follows:

1. Subject–bridge.
2. Bridge–predicate.
_____

3. Therefore, subject–predicate.

In syllogistic theory, the bridge is called the 'middle term'. The **middle term** simply serves to connect the subject to the predicate. It disappears in the conclusion. For example:

1. Cockroaches are insects.
2. Insects are good pets.
_____

3. Therefore, cockroaches are good pets.

Although, technically, each of the three statements in the syllo-gism has its own subject and predicate, we consider the subject and predicate that appears in the conclusion to be the overrid-ing subject and predicate for the syllogism as a whole. So, for this syllogism, 'Cockroaches' is the subject, 'are good pets' is the predicate, and 'insects' is the middle term, which serves to connect the subject to the predicate.

The categories described in categorical syllogisms can be thought of in terms of sets and subsets. The above syllogism asserts that the set of cockroaches is a subset of the set of insects, which is in turn a subset of the set of good pets.

By extension, a categorical statement might assert a relationship between a single individual and a category. For example:

Harvey is an insect.

This statement says Harvey belongs to the category of insects. In other words, Harvey the one-member set is a subset of the set of insects.

There are four different types of categorical statements that correspond to the four different ways we can relate one category to another. Aristotle assigned a name to each as follows:

All Xs are Y.		Universal affirmative
All Xs are not-Y.	(No X is Y)	Universal negative
Some Xs are Y.		Particular affirmative
Some Xs are not-Y.		Particular negative

By using these four different types of categorical statements as premises and conclusions we can produce a large variety of different syllogisms.

For a sampling of the possible combinations, let's use our universal affirmative categorical statement about Harvey, 'Harvey is an insect', as premise 1 of a syllogism:

1. Harvey is an insect.
2.

---

3. Therefore,

By inserting each of the four different types of categorical statements into premise 2 in turn, we can produce four different results.

First, we can insert a universal affirmative statement into premise 2, producing a universal affirmative statement in the conclusion, as follows:

1. Harvey is an insect.
2. All insects are good pets.

---

3. Therefore, Harvey is a good pet.

This is a deductively valid argument. We can prove its validity by drawing a diagram to represent it. Premise 1 states that the one-member set of Harvey (H) is a subset of the set of insects (I):

Premise 2 states that the set of insects is a subset of the set of good pets (G):

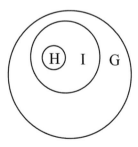

Now, without adding anything further to the picture, the conclusion is already there: Harvey is a subset of the set of good pets. If he is a subset of the set of insects and the set of insects is a subset of the set of good pets, then he *has to be* a subset of the set of good pets. The diagram proves that the conclusion necessarily follows from the premises.

Second, we could replace the universal affirmative statement in premise 2 with its opposite: a universal negative. Then we would have the following syllogism:

1. Harvey is an insect.
2. No insects are good pets.

_____

3. Therefore, Harvey is not a good pet.

This is also a deductively valid argument and we can prove it with a diagram. Premise 1 is the same as before:

Premise 2, however, tells us that the set of insects and the set of good pets do not intersect at all. We can represent this as follows:

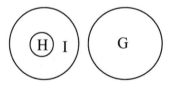

Once again, without adding anything further to the picture, the conclusion is already present: Harvey is not a subset of the set of good pets. If he is a member of the set of insects and the set of insects does not intersect with the set of good pets, then he *can't be* a good pet. The premises necessarily imply the conclusion.

So, the first two types of categorical statements, the universal affirmative and the universal negative, will work as the second premise of our syllogism about Harvey. But the same does not hold for the two remaining types of categorical statements.

In the third case, if we insert the particular affirmative statement 'Some insects are good pets', we generate the following steps:

1. Harvey is an insect.
2. Some insects are good pets.

<hr>

3. Therefore,?

We cannot complete the syllogism because nothing follows from these premises.

The problem with this argument becomes evident when we try to draw the diagram. Premise 1 gives us the same familiar configuration:

Premise 2 informs us that the circle we draw for (G) should overlap with the circle for (I) in some way. It does not tell us, however, whether Harvey lies inside or outside the overlapping area.

If Harvey lies inside the overlapping area, then the diagram will look like this:

According to this diagram, Harvey is a subset of the set of good pets.

If Harvey lies outside the overlapping area, however, then the diagram will look like this:

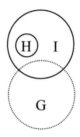

According to this diagram, Harvey is *not* a subset of the set of good pets.

In these two diagrams, we used a dotted line for the circle around (G) to indicate that the premises do not tell us how to draw it. Either diagram could be correct based on the information steps 1 and 2 provide. As a result, the conclusion is uncertain. And uncertainty is not permitted in the conclusion of deductive arguments! So we cannot draw any valid inference in this third syllogism about Harvey.

A similar problem occurs in the fourth case, when we insert the particular negative statement 'Some insects are not good pets', in place of premise 2:

1. Harvey is an insect.
2. Some insects are not good pets.

_____

3. Therefore,?

We cannot complete the syllogism because nothing follows from these premises.

Let's try to draw the diagram so we can see why. Premise 1 informs us that Harvey is a subset of the set of insects as before:

Premise 2 informs us that some members of the set of good pets are not members of the set of insects. This could mean that some members of the set of good pets are members of the set of insects and that Harvey is one of them. This interpretation is captured in the following diagram:

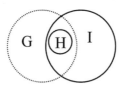

But premise 2 could just as easily mean that, while some members of the set of good pets are members of the set of insects, Harvey is not included among them. This interpretation is captured in the following diagram:

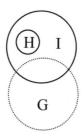

Just as before, the premises give us no basis for deciding which of these interpretations is correct.

Worse yet, there is a third interpretation to worry about as well. Premise 2 tells us that some insects are not good pets, but it never actually tells us that some insects *are* good pets. Normally, the phrase 'some aren't' implies 'some are'. But not always!

Imagine encountering an armadillo for the first time in your life and it tries to bite you. Someone asks you about your experience, and you say, 'Some armadillos aren't very nice'. Since you have never encountered any other armadillos, you may not be willing to grant that some armadillos *are* nice. All you know is that some aren't. There may not be any at all that are. So saying 'some aren't' does not necessarily imply 'some are'. (For the same reason 'some are' doesn't necessarily imply 'some aren't'.)

What this means for the case at hand is that premise 2, 'Some insects are not good pets', does not necessarily entitle us to assume that the set of good pets intersects with the set of insects. The diagram could look like this:

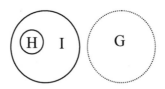

This interpretation would definitely imply that Harvey is not a member of the set of good pets. But this interpretation is just as uncertain as the other two!

So, in short, our fourth combination of premises leaves us without any conclusion to draw about Harvey. This is to say it does not make a valid syllogism.

By keeping premise 1 the same in each of our four syllogisms, we sampled just four possible combinations. But premise

1 can be any of the four different types of categorical statements as well. Moreover, there are different ways of connecting subjects and predicates to middle terms. When we calculate all the possible combinations, it turns out there are a total of 256 different types of categorical syllogisms! Nevertheless, only fifteen of them are valid.

Aristotle's successors wanted an easy way to determine whether or not a given argument was one of the fifteen valid syllogisms. They assigned a different vowel to each type of categorical statement as follows:

A	All Xs are Y.		Universal affirmative
E	All Xs are not-Y.	(No X is Y)	Universal negative
I	Some Xs are Y.		Particular affirmative
O	Some Xs are not-Y.		Particular negative.

Each of the three steps of a syllogism has to be one of these four types of categorical statement. Hence, each of the three steps can be labeled with one of the letters A, E, I, or O. This means every syllogism will have a label made up of three letters.

For example, a syllogism that uses universal affirmative statements in all three steps would be AAA. A syllogism that uses a universal negative in the first step, a universal affirmative in the second step, and a universal negative in the last step would be EAE.

Because it is tedious to keep track of three-letter designations, however, logicians expanded them into real names composed of three syllables. For example, 'AAA' became 'BARBARA' while 'EAE' became 'CELARENT,' etc. This makes it easier to recognize the fifteen valid categorical syllogisms.

The fifteen valid categorical syllogisms

Below are the fifteen valid categorical syllogisms filled out with content about animals. You can replace this content with any content you like and still have a valid argument as long as you follow the sequence of categorical statements indicated in the syllogism's name.

See if you can draw circle diagrams for each of the syllogisms. Use the first letter of the category named in the subject, predicate, and middle terms to label each circle. (If two categories start with the same letter, pick a different letter for one of them.) Draw a circle as a dotted line if the premise allows for more than one way to draw it. Start with the first premise, add the second premise, and – presto! – the conclusion should already be there. Given the premises, it is not possible to escape the conclusion – that's how we know these arguments are valid. You will find correctly drawn diagrams for these syllogisms in the answer key at the back of this book.

Barbara (AAA)

1. All dogs are mammals.
2. All mammals are animals.

3. Therefore, all dogs are animals.

Celarent (EAE)

1. No dogs have wings.
2. All poodles are dogs.

3. Therefore, no poodles have wings.

Darii (AII)

1. All dogs are colorblind.
2. Some pets are dogs.

___

3. Therefore, some pets are colorblind.

Ferio (EIO)

1. No dog is able to drive a car.
2. Some members of the police force are dogs.

___

3. Therefore, some members of the police force are not able to drive a car.

Cesare (EAE)

1. No dog-lover is sentimental.
2. All cat-lovers are sentimental.

___

3. Therefore, no cat-lover is a dog-lover.

Camestres (AEE)

1. All cats have fur.
2. No iguanas have fur.

___

3. Therefore, no iguanas are cats.

Festino (EIO)

1. No cat can talk.
2. Some of the critters in these boxes can talk.

___

3. Therefore, some of the critters in these boxes are not cats.

Baroco (AOO)

1. All good pets are lovable.
2. Some cats are not lovable.

   _____

3. Therefore, some cats are not good pets.

Disamis (IAI)

1. Some iguanas are beautiful.
2. All iguanas are lizards.

   _____

3. Therefore, some lizards are beautiful.

Datisi (AII)

1. All the dogs on this farm are collies.
2. Some of the dogs on this farm are feral.

   _____

3. Therefore, some collies are feral.

Bocardo (OAO)

1. Some cats do not eat meat.
2. All cats are mammals.

   _____

3. Therefore, some mammals do not eat meat.

Ferison (EIO)

1. No leash works on a snake.
2. Some leashes are guaranteed to work on any animal.

   _____

3. Therefore, some things that are guaranteed to work on any animal do not work on snakes.

Camenes (AEE)

1. All animal trainers have to be patient.
2. No one who is patient is a jerk.

---

3. Therefore, no jerks are animal trainers.

Dimaris (IAI)

1. Some lizards dwell in the desert.
2. All desert-dwellers are victims of global warming.

---

3. Therefore, some victims of global warming are lizards.

Fresison (EIO)

1. No animal lover is going to vote for this policy.
2. Some of those who are going to vote for this policy are farmers.

---

3. Therefore, some farmers are not animal lovers.

In each syllogism, the conclusion always determines which terms will be considered the overriding subject and predicate for the syllogism. The remaining term, which will appear twice in the premises but disappear from the conclusion, is the middle term. In the case of Barbara, the middle term is literally in the middle:

1. Subject-middle.
2. Middle-predicate.

---

3. Therefore, subject-predicate.

But the middle term doesn't need to be literally in the middle to do its work as a disappearing bridge. In fact, moving the middle term around is partly how we generate so many different syllogisms. Have another look at our example for Bocardo:

1. Some cats do not eat meat.
2. All cats are mammals.

---

3. Therefore, some mammals do not eat meat.

Its conclusion tells us that 'mammals' is the subject for the syllogism and 'do not eat meat' is the predicate. This means it conforms to the following pattern:

1. Middle–predicate.
2. Middle–subject.

---

3. Therefore, subject–predicate.

Even if you switched the order of the premises (which would do no harm to the inference) the middle term still would not be in the middle. But it doesn't matter, because it still forms an effective bridge.

It may feel a bit overwhelming to think that there are fifteen different valid syllogisms out there for you to be aware of as a critical thinker. Don't worry. Barbara is by far the most common. The main thing is for you to be able to identify transitive links in the arguments you read. Let's try this now.

Opposite is a passage by renowned American psychologist B. F. Skinner, from the introduction to his utopian novel, *Walden Two*.

Skinner devotes this passage to arguing that the great cultural revolution we need will not come about through political action.

The syllogistic quality of this passage is not immediately evident. Looking at the last paragraph, however, it becomes clear that Skinner's argument hinges on his effort to carve out and dissociate two different categories of individuals: the great men of history (G) and the political leaders (P). We can draw these sets as follows:

HOW TO BRING ABOUT A CULTURAL REVOLUTION

Suppose we do know what is needed for the good life; how are we to bring it about? In America we almost instinctively move to change things by political action: we pass laws, we vote for new leaders. But a good many people are beginning to wonder. They have lost faith in a democratic process in which the so-called will of the people is obviously controlled in undemocratic ways. And there is always the question whether a government based on punitive sanctions is inappropriate if we are to solve problems nonpunitively.

It has been argued that the solution might be socialism, but it has often been pointed out that socialism, like capitalism, is committed to growth, and hence to over consumption and pollution. Certainly Russia after fifty years is not a model we wish to emulate. China may be closer to the solutions I have been talking about, but a Communist revolution in America is hard to imagine. It would be a bloody affair, and there is always Lenin's question to be answered: how much suffering can one impose upon those now living for the sake of those who will follow? And can we be sure that those who follow will be any better off?

Fortunately, there is another possibility. An important theme in *Walden Two* is that political action is to be avoided. Historians have stopped writing about wars and conquering heroes and empires and what they have turned to instead, though far less dramatic, is far more important. The great cultural revolutions have not started with politics. The great men who are said to have made a difference in human affairs – Confucius, Buddha, Jesus, the scholars and scientists of the Revival of Learning, the leaders of the Enlightenment, Marx – were not political leaders. They did not change history by running for office. We need not aspire to their eminence in order to profit from their example.

B. F. Skinner, 'Walden Two Revisited', in *Walden Two* (New York: Macmillan, 1976), pp. xvi.

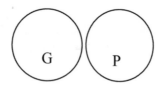

He then goes on to suggest that all successful revolutions (S) have been inspired by the great men of history, which we can add to the drawing as follows:

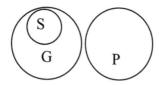

And without adding anything further we see that we are entitled to draw the inference that no successful revolution has been inspired by political leaders.

In other words, what we have is the following syllogism:

1. No great men are political.
2. All successful revolutions are inspired by great men.

3. Therefore, no successful revolutions are political.

This is a valid syllogism that conforms to the pattern of Celarent, as seen above:

1. No dogs have wings.   Middle-predicate
2. All poodles are dogs.   Subject-middle

3. Therefore, no poodles have wings.   Subject-predicate

If the premises are true, then the conclusion has to be true.

While our syllogistic reconstruction of Skinner's argument greatly simplifies the passage, it is nevertheless very useful for two reasons.

First of all, it helps us understand what Skinner is saying. Naturally, there may be some disagreement over exactly how to interpret the passage as a whole. Nevertheless, our interpretation is defensible and crystallizes Skinner's point.

Second, reconstructing the argument syllogistically puts us in a good position to evaluate it. Some might object to premise 1 by presenting examples of great men of history who were political leaders. Or they might object that the great men Skinner himself names were in fact political leaders. Others might accept premise 1 while rejecting premise 2. They might argue that successful revolutions are inspired, not by great men, but by advances in technology or by God. We could go on at length about the many interesting things that could be said both for and against the premises.

For present purposes, however, the important thing to see is how Aristotle's theory of the syllogism got us started. It provided a reliable framework for organizing our analysis of Skinner's argument.

Syllogisms will not leap off the page at you. You have to dig a bit for associations and dissociations in the author's reasoning. With practice you can recognize the patterns more easily. Ultimately, though, the crucial importance of Aristotle's theory of the syllogism is transitivity. When all else fails, you can almost always find the familiar chain:

1. X is Y.
2. Y is Z.

_____

3. Therefore, X is Z.

In the end, that's all Skinner's argument amounts to: successful revolutions are inspired by great men and great men are not political; therefore, successful revolutions are not political. Nothing fancy needed. But being able to identify and avoid errors in transitivity is the foundation of critical thinking.

Five common errors in syllogistic reasoning

Although syllogistic reasoning comes naturally to human beings, we are also prone to certain syllogistic errors, sometimes called 'fallacies'. A **fallacy** is any mistake in reasoning. Since you can't avoid them if you don't know about them, we will pause here to go over the top five.

1. Undistributed middle

In this fallacy, neither of the premises accounts for all members of the category described by the middle term. As a result, the middle term fails to link the subject and predicate term.

For example, suppose you meet a man named Jerry at a cocktail party. When he takes a swig of his drink, his jacket comes open a bit and you notice he's wearing a gun in a shoulder holster. The following reasoning might flash through your mind:

1. All undercover cops carry a gun.
2. Jerry carries a gun.

---

3. Therefore, Jerry is an undercover cop.

Later you might tell a friend that there was an undercover cop at the party. Looking at the reasoning laid out in standard form, however, it becomes evident that your conclusion does not follow from your premises.

As mentioned above, the conclusion always determines which terms will be considered the overriding subject and predicate for the syllogism. So we know that Jerry is the subject of this syllogism and 'is an undercover cop' is the predicate. Copying this designation into the premises, we can label the argument as follows:

1. Predicate-middle.
2. Subject-middle.

---

3. Therefore, subject-predicate.

The term 'carries a gun' is the middle term because it is supposed to be the disappearing bridge. But in this case, it fails to do the job. This pattern of reasoning will always be invalid.

If you tried to draw a diagram for it, you would see the problem immediately. The first premise can be represented like this:

It tells you that the set of undercover cops is a subset of the set of gun carriers.

But how will you add the second premise? It tells you Jerry is a one-member subset of the set of gun carriers. So you know a circle labeled 'J' must be inserted in (G). But you don't know whether the circle labeled 'J' should go inside or outside (U).

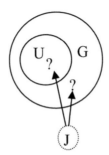

The conclusion of the argument unjustifiably *assumes* that (J) should go inside (U). And that's why the argument is invalid.

The technical way to put the point is that the middle term is not distributed. A term is considered 'distributed' when all individual members of the category it describes are accounted for. Our cop syllogism commits the fallacy of the undistributed middle because it does not give us an account of all of the members of the category 'gun carrier'.

In order to make the argument valid, the first premise would have to say '*Only* undercover cops carry a gun'. In other words, it would need to reverse the middle term and the predicate as follows: 'All gun carriers are undercover cops.' This would give us a full account of the middle term because it would tell us that the set of gun carriers is a subset of the set of undercover cops. Then the fact that Jerry was a member of the set of gun carriers would necessarily land him in the set of undercover cops. (But then, of course, the first premise would be false because it simply isn't true that all gun carriers are undercover cops.)

2. Illicit treatment of the predicate term

In this fallacy, the premise containing the syllogism's predicate term fails to account for all the members of the category which that predicate term describes. Consider the following example:

1. All police officers are brave.   Middle-predicate
2. No criminals are police officers.   Subject-middle
    ─────────────────────────────   ──────────────
3. Therefore, no criminals are brave.   Subject-predicate

The second premise of this argument dissociates the set of criminals from the set of police officers. But we cannot be sure whether or not the set of criminals lies outside the category described by the predicate term 'brave'.

If you tried to draw a diagram for this argument you would begin with the first premise as follows:

The second premise instructs you to draw a circle outside of (P) for the set of criminals, (C). But should (C) go inside or outside of (B)?

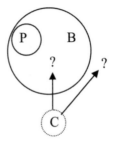

We don't know. The conclusion unjustifiably *assumes* it should go outside of (B). And this is why the conclusion does not follow.

3. Illicit treatment of the subject term

In this fallacy, the same problem we saw above occurs in the premise containing the syllogism's subject term. Consider the following example:

1. All criminals are dangerous.	Middle-predicate
2. All criminals are interesting.	Middle-subject
3. Therefore, all interesting people are dangerous.	Subject-predicate

The first premise tells us the set of criminals is a subset of the set of dangerous people. We could draw this as follows:

The second premise tells us the set of criminals is also a subset of the set of interesting people. We could draw this as follows:

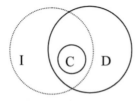

But the conclusion of the syllogism tells us that the circle for (I) is supposed to be entirely contained within the circle for (D). This is something that the premises did not guarantee. Hence, the conclusion makes an invalid inference.

4. Exclusive premises

In this fallacy, both premises are negative. As a result, no link is established between the subject and predicate terms. Consider the following example:

1. No dangerous people are invited   Predicate-middle
    to the party.
2. Some people who are invited to the   Middle-subject
    party are not spies.

---

3. Therefore, some spies are not   Subject-predicate
    dangerous people.

It is obvious at a glance that there are just too many negatives in this line of reasoning. Hopefully, you will never run into such an awkward argument!

The problem with the inference is once again proven in the diagram. The first premise tells us that the set of dangerous people does not intersect with the set of people invited to the party. We can draw this as follows:

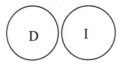

The second premise tells us that the set of people invited to the party is not a subset of the set of spies. It is tempting to add a circle for 'spies' that partially intersects with (I) as follows:

This diagram does imply the conclusion that some spies are not dangerous people. Nevertheless, the second premise gives us no justification for drawing (S) as we did.

Although the second premise asserts that some spies are not invited to the party, it does not assert that some *are*. The assertion that some spies are not invited to the party is consistent with the assertion that *no* spies are invited to the party. (Recall our discussion of the unfriendly armadillo, above.) So it is possible that (S) is actually a subset of the set of dangerous people. In other words, we could just as easily add the second premise as follows:

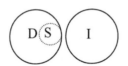

In this case, the conclusion would be false. Recall that, according to the definition of validity, an argument is valid if and only if there is no possible way for the premises to be true while the conclusion is false. We have found a way to make the premises true while the conclusion is false; therefore, the argument is invalid.

5. Affirmative from a negative

In this fallacy, the conclusion attempts to draw an affirmative conclusion from a negative premise. For example:

1. No spies are honorable.   Subject-middle
2. No honorable people deserve to be shot.   Middle-predicate

---

3. Therefore, all spies deserve to be shot.   Subject-predicate

The first premise tells us that the set of spies does not intersect with the set of honorable people. We can draw this as follows:

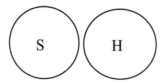

The second premise tells us that the set of honorable people does not intersect with the set of people who deserve to be shot (D). But we really are in no position to add (D) to the diagram because we have no idea how it relates to (S).

(D) could intersect with (S):

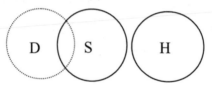

Or (D) could be a subset of (S):

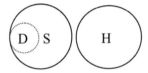

Or (S) could be a subset of (D):

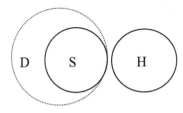

The conclusion *assumes* the last of these possibilities with no justification.

The easiest way to avoid this fallacy is to remember that, if either premise is negative, the conclusion must also be negative.

That's enough of Aristotle's theory of the categorical syllogism! Working through these inferences and drawing the diagrams to represent them will help to sharpen your logic skills. While it is not important to memorize the fifteen valid syllogisms or the five most common syllogistic fallacies, it is important to see how the former preserve validity while the latter destroy it. Once you have mastered the concept of validity you will be able to move beyond categorical syllogisms to more sophisticated argument forms, as we shall see in the next chapter.

Exercises

Identify 'Barbara' syllogisms underlying the arguments in the following passages. Reconstruct them in valid (deductive) standard form using this pattern:

1. Subject–bridge.
2. Bridge–predicate.

   _____

3. Therefore, subject–predicate.

Follow these five steps for success:

(1) Draw a blank, three-step standard form:
   1.
   2.

   _____

   3. Therefore,
(2) Fill in the conclusion with a categorical statement containing a clear subject and predicate. Remember that the conclusion is the main thing the author is trying to prove to you.
   1.
   2.

   _____

   3. Therefore, S is P.
(3) Copy S to its proper position in premise 1 and P to its proper position in premise 2:
   1. S is _____.
   2. _____is P.

   _____

   3. Therefore, S is P.
(4) Find the bridge or middle term that connects the subject to the predicate.
   1. S is M.
   2. M is P.

   _____

   3. Therefore, S is P.
(5) As always, feel free to translate the author's ideas into your own words and remember there is more than one way to do it. To check your work, draw circle diagrams to represent

your syllogisms and then compare your answers to the answers in the key at the back of this book.

Classics

It was noted at the start of the chapter that Athens was at war for almost the entire period of the democracy. The basic divisions of the citizen-body, the ten tribes, were, as we have seen, military units, and to be a citizen was to be a soldier. Studies of the Athenian democracy which concentrate on the internal workings of the city in peacetime ignore the areas of life that have the most importance for the citizens themselves. Farming and fighting were the most common activities of Athenian citizens, something very different from the experience of the inhabitants of modern democracies. Concern for the gods was important in both these activities, and therefore central to the lives of the people of democratic Athens.

> Hugh Bowden, *Classical Athens and the Delphic Oracle:*
> *Divination and Democracy* (Cambridge:
> Cambridge University Press, 2005), p. 151.

Philosophy

Find two linked syllogisms.

Now he who exercises his reason and cultivates it seems to be both in the best state of mind and most dear to the gods. For if the gods have any care for human affairs, as they are thought to have, it would be reasonable both that they should delight in that which was best and most akin to them (i.e. reason) and that they should reward those who love and honor this most, as caring for the things that are dear to them and acting both rightly and nobly. And that all these attributes belong most of all to the philosopher is manifest. He, therefore, is the dearest to the gods. And he who is that will presumably be also the happiest; so that in this way too the philosopher will more than any other be happy.

Aristotle, *Nicomachean Ethics*, trans. W. D. Ross, in *The Basic Works of Aristotle*, ed. Richard McKeon (New York: Random House, 1941), p. 1108

Religion

Find two linked syllogisms.

Perhaps the antagonism between sex and religion can be traced to sex's linkage with the body. Many religions seek to commune with and emphasize the eternal, the immortal, the everlasting. The body is none of these things; the body decays, withers, dies, and eventually rots. Therefore, many religions see the body as impermanent and thus of lesser value than the soul, which is understood as eternal and transcendent. Anything associated with the body is subsequently deemed not only of less importance, but often unholy. Sex, of course, is deeply associated with the body. In fact, the body is its universe. Because most religions focus on the eternal, and because the body is not eternal, and because sex is ultimately a celebration of the body, it perhaps makes sense that religions would develop a hostility toward sexual activity, envisioning it as a feast of the impermanent, an indulgence of the transitory. As Paul writes in Romans 8:13, 'For if you live by the flesh, you will die'.

Christel Manning and Phil Zuckerman, *Sex and Religion* (Belmont, CA: Wadsworth, 2005), p. 11

3

Sentential logic

Put the argument into a concrete shape, into an image, some hard phrase, round and solid as a ball, which they can see and handle and carry home with them, and the cause is half won.

Ralph Waldo Emerson

As we have seen, a categorical statement asserts a relationship between two categories. The classic example of a categorical statement is:

All men are mortal.

This statement asserts that every member of the set of men is a member of the set of mortal beings – men are not immortal like the gods.

Throughout history since Aristotle's day, this classic categorical statement has been used to illustrate syllogistic logic:

1. All men are mortal.
2. Socrates is a man.

---

3. Therefore, Socrates is mortal.

If the premises are true, then the conclusion cannot be false.

Categorical syllogisms demonstrate the connections between categorical statements. Although this alone does a great deal to clarify thought, logicians were not long satisfied limiting themselves to categorical statements. Nor will you, as a critical thinker, be satisfied with this limitation. You will want to be able to demonstrate connections between categorical statements and other kinds of statements. This brings us to sentential logic.

Sentential logic, also known as 'propositional logic', studies the connections between different kinds of statements.

Conditional statements

The pivotal concept for sentential logic is the conditional statement, which is a very common component in the arguments we use every day. A **conditional statement** is a statement of the form 'If . . . then . . .' The 'If' part of a conditional statement is called the **antecedent** and the 'then' part is called the **consequent**.

Consider the following example about Socrates's dog, Argos:

If Socrates is mortal, then Argos is mortal.

This statement uses the logical operator 'If . . . then . . .' to connect two categorical statements. The antecedent contains the categorical statement 'Socrates is mortal' while the consequent contains the categorical statement 'Argos is mortal'.

The logical operator 'If . . . then . . .' asserts a relationship between the two categorical statements: it asserts that the truth of the second categorical statement is implied by the truth of the first categorical statement. This is to say that, given the truth of the antecedent, the consequent must be true as well. If the antecedent is *not* true then we don't know whether the consequent is true or false. But if the antecedent is true, then the consequent must be true as well.

(You may notice that this relationship is parallel to the definition of a valid argument: if the premises are true then the conclusion must be true as well. This parallel is no coincidence. The conditional statement asserts logical implication in the same way a deductive argument does.)

Both components of our conditional statement about Socrates and his dog are categorical statements: the antecedent, 'Socrates is mortal', tells us that Socrates is a member of the category of mortals; the consequent, 'Argos is mortal', tells us that Argos is a member of the category of mortals. By describing membership in categories, categorical statements attempt to convey facts. Even a false categorical statement, such as 'Socrates is a woman', is *attempting* to convey a fact. This is to say that categorical statements are **descriptive statements**.

The really great thing about conditional statements is that they don't only connect descriptive statements. They can connect any two kinds of statements you like. For critical thinkers, the most important type of statement next to the descriptive statement is the prescriptive statement, also known as the normative statement. While a descriptive statement tells how the world *is*, a **prescriptive statement** tells how the world *should be*. For example:

Socrates should make every day count.

This statement conveys a value judgment rather than a fact. It is not descriptive but prescriptive.

Needless to say, prescriptive statements are very common. Here are some examples we have already encountered in previous chapters:

'Vincent Cockley should receive the maximum penalty.'
'I should buy a hybrid.'
'The desire for sexual expression should be given an outlet through transmutation.'
'Roe v. Wade and the Abortion Act should be repealed.'

Bear in mind that there are various synonyms for 'should', such as 'ought to', 'must', 'would be best', etc. Prescriptive statements can be negative as well, as in 'should not', 'ought not', 'must not', 'would be wrong', etc.

It is important to be able to identify prescriptive statements because they often serve as the main proposal of an author's argument – the conclusion he or she is trying to establish.

The conditional operator 'If . . . then . . .' can connect a descriptive statement to a prescriptive statement as follows:

If Socrates is mortal, then he should make every day count.

It can also connect two prescriptive statements. For example:

If Socrates should make every day count, then Argos should make every day count, too.

While it is not impossible to incorporate prescriptive elements into categorical syllogisms, sentential logic and the conditional operator 'If . . . then . . .' provide a more natural vehicle for prescriptive arguments.

Another type of statement the conditional operator can connect is the predictive statement. A **predictive statement** tells how the world *will be*. For example:

Socrates will die of cancer within six months.

A predictive statement is really just a descriptive statement about the future. Scientists often make predictive statements. For example, a physician might present an argument for his conclusion that Socrates will die of cancer within six months. Nevertheless, non-scientific arguments often incorporate predictive statements as well. For example,

If Socrates will die of cancer within six months, then he should be allowed to retire now and receive a government pension.

Here, the predictive statement provides a condition for a prescriptive statement. We can easily imagine a lawyer or a philosopher using this conditional statement in an argument.

One last type of statement worth mentioning here is the counterfactual conditional. A **counterfactual-conditional statement** tells how the world *would be* if its antecedent were true. For example:

If Socrates were a god, then he would be immortal.

This statement does not assert that Socrates *is* immortal, that he *should be* immortal, or that he *will be* immortal. Rather, it asserts that he *would be* immortal if the world were different – if he were a god instead of a man.

Counterfactual conditionals are very useful in arguments, especially when criticizing an opponent. For example, someone might assert,

> If Socrates were allowed to retire now and receive a government pension, then everyone else with cancer would be allowed to do the same, and the government would go broke.

This counterfactual conditional advances a consideration against the prescriptive statement presented above.

As a critical thinker, you will encounter arguments involving categorical statements, conditional statements, prescriptive statements, predictive statements, and counterfactual conditional statements. Sentential logic's rules of inference will help you put them in order.

Rules of inference

Although there are unlimited ways to make good arguments using different kinds of statements, six main patterns appear repeatedly. It pays to learn these patterns so that you can recognize them when you see them and use them in making arguments of your own.

Hypothetical syllogism

The rule of inference known as 'hypothetical syllogism' is a straightforward application of the same transitive reasoning we have seen before. Recall that the following is the simplest example of transitivity:

1. X is Y.
2. Y is Z.

---

3. Therefore, X is Z.

The variable 'Y' is the bridge between 'X' and 'Z'. If X is Y and Y is Z, then X must be Z. This is a deductively valid standard form argument.

Suppose you are a detective trying to solve the murder of Cassandra Thomas, the owner of a grocery store in Gamerton who was shot dead on the night of 10 July. You have two suspects: Vincent Cockley and Mark Deal. You interview a teenager named Dawn Rummy who swears she saw Mark do it. You therefore reason as follows:

1. If Dawn is telling the truth, then Mark is the killer.
2. If Mark is the killer, then Vincent is innocent.

---

3. Therefore, if Dawn is telling the truth, then Vincent is innocent.

This is a hypothetical syllogism. It is transitive reasoning because the premises form a sequence such that the middle member of the sequence makes a bridge from the first member to the last. The difference between hypothetical syllogisms and the categorical syllogisms we studied in the last chapter is that the members of the sequence in hypothetical syllogisms are whole statements rather than just subject and predicate terms as they are in categorical syllogisms.

We can symbolize our hypothetical syllogism about the murder of Cassandra Thomas as follows:

Let A = Dawn
Let B = telling the truth
Let C = Mark

Let D = the killer
Let E = Vincent
Let F = Innocent

1. If (A is B), then (C is D).
2. If (C is D), then (E is F).

---

3. Therefore, if (A is B), then (E is F).

The statement (C is D) acts as a bridge linking the statement (A is B) with the statement (E is F).

Since whole statements, rather than subjects and predicates, are treated as the primary units in sentential logic, logicians often use single capital letters to represent them. In fact, they have designated the capital letters P, Q, R, and S to serve as the standard symbols for sentential units. Hence, the standard symbolic representation of the hypothetical syllogism is as follows:

1. If P, then Q.
2. If Q, then R.

---

3. Therefore, if P, then R.

Just remember: you must plug a whole statement into each variable, and you must use the same statement for the same variable. You can use any statement you want – categorical, prescriptive, predictive, counterfactual – the results will be valid as long as you follow the pattern exactly.

Hypothetical syllogism is a good rule of inference to use in cases where the conclusion depends on an unknown factor. In our example above, we were not able to conclude that Vincent is innocent but only that *if Dawn is telling the truth*, then he is innocent. Hypothetical syllogism is called 'hypothetical' because it leaves you with a big 'if' in the conclusion.

Modus ponens

The rule of inference known as 'modus ponens' is like hypothetical syllogism except it allows you to eliminate the 'if' and come to a definite conclusion.

Suppose Dawn passes a lie detector test when she testifies that she saw Mark shoot Cassandra. You may now modify your original reasoning as follows:

1. If Dawn is telling the truth, then Vincent is innocent.
2. Dawn is telling the truth (because she passed the lie detector test).

---

3. Therefore, Vincent is innocent.

Now you have a definite conclusion – no ifs about it.

Recall that every conditional statement has two components: the 'if' part is called the antecedent while the 'then' part is called the consequent. Modus ponens works by asserting a conditional statement in the first premise and then proceeding to affirm its antecedent in the second premise. This entitles you to infer the truth of the consequent in the conclusion.

In fact, the name 'modus ponens' is Latin shorthand for 'the method of affirming the antecedent'. The symbolic representation for modus ponens is as follows:

1. If P, then Q.
2. P.

---

3. Therefore, Q.

This pattern of reasoning is always valid. Although the conditional statement usually comes in the first premise and the affirmation of its antecedent in the second, you can switch the order of the premises and it won't make any difference.

The fallacy of affirming the consequent

While switching the order of the premises in a modus ponens argument doesn't make any difference, switching the order of the *variables* (P and Q) makes a huge difference. Modus ponens has an evil twin called 'the fallacy of affirming the consequent'. It comes from switching the order of the Ps and Qs and it instantly destroys the argument. Because this fallacy looks a lot like modus ponens it is easy to make the mistake of thinking it is valid. But it isn't and it is absolutely crucial that you understand why.

Suppose Dawn declines to take the lie detector test, leaving you unable to confirm what she said about seeing Mark shoot Cassandra. So, instead, you check out Vincent's alibi. He claims he was at the pub next door paying for his supper when the gun went off. After hearing Vincent's story, you check with the waitress at the pub, and, sure enough, she confirms that Vincent was paying for his supper when they both heard the shot.

Upon gaining this information, you may be tempted to modify your original reasoning as follows:

1. If Dawn is telling the truth (about seeing Mark shoot Cassandra), then Vincent is innocent.
2. Vincent is innocent (because he was with the waitress when the shot went off).

---

3. Therefore, Dawn is telling the truth (about seeing Mark shoot Cassandra).

Although this reasoning may seem right, it isn't. Its structure can be symbolized as follows:

1. If P, then Q.
2. Q.

---

3. Therefore, P.

It is called 'the fallacy of affirming the consequent' because the variables have been switched: step 2 affirms the *consequent* of the conditional in step 1 (Q) instead of affirming its *antecedent* (P).

If you stop to think about it, you can see why the argument is invalid. Just because the shooter couldn't have been Vincent doesn't mean it was Mark. Perhaps Dawn hates Mark and lied about seeing him pull the trigger. Or perhaps she mistook someone else for him. The bottom line is that while proving Mark did it would get Vincent off the hook, the reverse is not true: proving Vincent didn't do it does not guarantee Mark did.

As a critical thinker, you must resist the temptation to commit the fallacy of affirming the consequent at all costs. There is, however, a valid way of reversing a modus ponens argument. It is called modus tollens.

Modus tollens

The rule of inference known as 'modus tollens' allows you to deny the consequent of a conditional statement and thereby conclude that its antecedent is not true. We can illustrate this point by extending our story.

Now that Vincent is off the hook, you need to find out whether or not it was Mark. So you check out his alibi. He claims to have been at a hotel in Moscow when the murder occurred. So, you go to Moscow with a picture of Mark and ask the clerks at the hotel whether they can confirm that he was there the afternoon of 10 July. One clerk confirms that he stopped by the front desk for a newspaper at noon that day. Taking account of the distance between Moscow and Gamerton, you calculate that it would have been physically impossible for Mark to make the trip in time to kill Cassandra. Hence, you may now modify your original reasoning as follows:

1. If Dawn is telling the truth, then Mark is the killer.

2. But Mark is not the killer (because he was in Moscow).

---

3. Therefore, Dawn is not telling the truth.

This is modus tollens. Its name is Latin shorthand for 'the method of denying the consequent'. You can see why: the first step asserts a conditional; the second step denies its consequent; the conclusion infers the denial of its antecedent.

The symbolic representation for modus tollens is as follows:

1. If P, then Q.
2. Not-Q.

---

3. Therefore, not-P.

This pattern of reasoning is always valid. Although the conditional statement usually comes first and the denial of the consequent second, you can switch the order of the premises and it won't make any difference.

The fallacy of denying the antecedent

Unfortunately, modus tollens has an evil twin as well. It's called 'the fallacy of denying the antecedent'. It comes from switching the order of the variables (P and Q) and it instantly destroys the validity of the argument.

Suppose you are unable to go to Moscow to check out Mark's alibi. So, instead, you decide to investigate Dawn's story. She claims she stopped by Cassandra's shop to buy cigarettes on her way home from school. She was in the bathroom when she heard shouting. As she came out, she saw Mark pull a gun from his coat and shoot Cassandra point blank. Although Dawn seems sincere, you learn from several of her fellow students that she was actually at a football game after school that day.

You may be tempted to modify your original reasoning as follows:

1. If Dawn is telling the truth, then Mark is the killer.
2. But Dawn is not telling the truth (because she was at a football game).

---

3. Therefore, Mark is not the killer.

While this reasoning may look right at first glance, it isn't. Its structure can be symbolized as follows:

1. If P, then Q.
2. Not-P.

---

3. Therefore, Not-Q.

It is called 'the fallacy of denying the antecedent' because the variables have been switched: step 2 denies the antecedent of the conditional in step 1 (P) instead of denying its consequent (Q).

On close inspection, you can see why the argument is invalid. Just because Dawn isn't telling the truth doesn't mean Mark is not the killer. Perhaps Dawn somehow knew Mark did it, even though she wasn't really there to witness it. The bottom line is that, if we were able to confirm that Dawn was telling the truth, then Mark would be busted, but the reverse is not true: disproving what Dawn said does not exonerate him.

As with the fallacy of affirming the consequent, critical thinkers must avoid committing the fallacy of denying the antecedent at all costs. One thing that makes it difficult to distinguish the two modus rules from their corresponding fallacies is that the antecedent and/or the consequent of the conditional may already be negative.

Suppose we were to start a standard form with the following conditional statement:

1. If Dawn was not at the shop, then she did not witness the shooting.

2. _____

3. Therefore,

How would you fill in step 2 and step 3 in order to make the argument modus ponens?

The answer is that you would have to affirm the antecedent in order to conclude that the consequent is true. But notice that, since the antecedent happens to be negative, affirming the antecedent will mean inserting a negative statement in step 2 (and likewise for step 3):

1. If Dawn was not at the shop, then she did not witness the shooting.
2. Dawn was not at the shop.
_____

3. Therefore, Dawn did not witness the shooting.

At a glance, this argument may look like the fallacy of denying the antecedent because premise 2 is negative. But it actually is a perfect instance of modus ponens. Modus ponens does not require that step 2 be positive but rather that it affirm the antecedent of the conditional statement in step 1, whether that antecedent be positive or negative.

The same point applies to modus tollens. Go back to our unfinished standard form starting with the following conditional statement:

1. If Dawn was not at the shop, then she did not witness the shooting.
2. _____

3. Therefore,

How would you fill in step 2 and step 3 in order to make the argument modus tollens?

The answer is that you would have to deny the consequent in order to conclude that the antecedent is false. But notice that, since the consequent is already negative, denying it will mean inserting a positive statement in step 2 (and likewise for step 3):

1. If Dawn was not at the shop, then she did not witness the shooting.
2. But Dawn did witness the shooting.

---

3. Therefore, Dawn was at the shop.

At a glance, this argument may look like the fallacy of affirming the consequent because premise 2 is positive. But it actually is a perfect instance of modus tollens. Modus tollens does not require that step 2 be negative but rather that it deny the consequent of the conditional statement in step 1, whether that consequent is positive or negative.

In short, the fallacies in question do not depend on whether step 2 is positive or negative – they depend on denying the antecedent or affirming the consequent. You need to be able to notice in an instant that these patterns of reasoning are illogical. If you do not yet see the difference between these fallacies and their brothers, modus ponens and modus tollens, make up some examples of your own and study them until you are thoroughly convinced.

Reductio ad absurdum

The whole point to learning rules of inference is to be able to defend your position on one side of a debate. The rule of inference known as 'reductio ad absurdum' is particularly useful in a direct confrontation with an opponent.

By now, everyone back at the police station has heard about the murder of Cassandra, and they're all taking sides. One side, the 'pro–Dawn' faction, insists that, although Dawn did stop by the football game, she left in time to witness the shooting at the shop. This faction argues using modus ponens as follows:

1. If Dawn is telling the truth, then Mark is the killer.
2. Dawn is telling the truth.

_____

3. Therefore, Mark is the killer.

The other side, the 'anti-Dawn' faction, insists that Mark's Moscow alibi exonerates him. They argue using modus tollens as follows:

1. If Dawn is telling the truth, then Mark is the killer.
2. Mark is not the killer.

_____

3. Therefore, Dawn is not telling the truth.

Notice that both sides agree about the first premise. Where they disagree is in the second premise, and this leads them to conflicting conclusions. This is why it is often said that 'one man's modus ponens is another man's modus tollens'.

Modus tollens is such a useful way to reverse an opponent's argument that the basic idea behind it has been expanded into a souped-up format known as reductio ad absurdum. In reductio ad absurdum, the goal is not just to reverse your opponent's argument, but to reduce it to an absurdity. Bear in mind, however, that to reduce an opponent's argument to absurdity does not mean to ridicule it. In logic, we use the term 'absurdity' to mean 'impossibility'. An impossibility is something that cannot be true. So, if you prove your opponent's view implies an 'absurdity', you've refuted it.

Reductio ad absurdum works by assuming for the sake of argument that the opponent's view is correct and then proceeding to show how this very assumption leads to an impossibility. For example, the anti-Dawn faction might argue as follows:
To prove: Dawn is not telling the truth.

1. Suppose Dawn were telling the truth.
2. If Dawn were telling the truth, then Mark would have had to travel from Moscow to Gamerton in less than six hours.
3. But it is absurd to suppose that someone can travel from Moscow to Gamerton in such a short amount of time.

---

4. Therefore, Dawn is not telling the truth.

Notice that the argument starts with a 'To prove' line. This signals to the reader that premise 1 of the argument is actually the opponent's view. Without this step, the reader might not realize premise 1 is only being proposed for the sake of argument. Notice also the use of the counterfactual conditional in premise 2. This signals that the antecedent of the conditional is contrary to fact.

It would be interesting to hear how the pro-Dawn faction would respond to this apparent absurdity. Perhaps they would use disjunctive syllogism.

Disjunctive syllogism

The rule of inference known as disjunctive syllogism proposes that the issue boils down to a choice between two possibilities and then rejects one of those possibilities in order to conclude that the other must be true.

Suppose the pro-Dawn faction points out that Mark could have paid the Moscow hotel clerk to say he stopped by the front desk for a newspaper at noon on 10 July even though he didn't. They then give Dawn a lie detector test that confirms her story to be true: she left the football game early and walked to Cassandra's store where she saw Mark shoot Cassandra from ten feet away. Armed with this evidence, the pro-Dawn faction may argue as follows:

1. Either Mark killed Cassandra or Dawn is mistaken.

2. Dawn could not be mistaken about a man who stood just ten feet away.

---

3. Therefore, Mark killed Cassandra.

This rule of inference is called 'disjunctive syllogism' because a disjunct is an 'either . . . or' statement.

The symbolic representation for disjunctive syllogism is as follows:

1. Either P or Q.
2. Not–Q.

---

3. Therefore, P.

This pattern of reasoning is always valid. Notice that you could just as easily substitute 'Not-P' in premise 2 and conclude with 'Therefore Q'. Unlike in the case of modus ponens and modus tollens, the order of the variables doesn't matter.

Disjunctive syllogism is a handy argument form. The only problem is that it requires being able to reduce the entire issue to just two possibilities, which is often difficult to do. In this case, for example, the pro-Dawn faction had to rule out the possibility that Dawn was lying before presenting the two remaining possibilities.

Of course, you can make a disjunctive syllogism with more than two disjuncts. Suppose you presented four possibilities and then proceeded to eliminate three so you were left with just one. In theory, there is no limit to the process of elimination. In practice, however, there will always be a limit and your opponent may complain you left the most important possibility out. This complaint amounts to a charge of the fallacy known as 'false dilemma', which we will examine in chapter 4.

In the case at hand, the anti-Dawn faction may argue it is not acceptable to rule out two other possibilities: that the lie detector test was faulty and that Dawn was on hallucinatory drugs. They could make their counterargument using constructive dilemma.

Constructive dilemma

The rule of inference known as constructive dilemma starts out just like disjunctive syllogism. Rather than eliminating one of the two possibilities, however, it draws implications from both and then ends with another disjunction.

The anti-Dawn faction may argue as follows:

1. It could be that the lie detector test was faulty or that Dawn was on hallucinatory drugs.
2. If the lie detector test was faulty, then Dawn could be lying.
3. If Dawn was on hallucinatory drugs, then she could be mistaken.

---

4. Therefore, Dawn could be lying or mistaken.

This pattern of reasoning is called 'constructive dilemma' because it takes you from one disjunction of possibilities to another disjunction of possibilities.

The symbolic representation for constructive dilemma is as follows:

1. Either P or Q.
2. If P, then R.
3. If Q, then S.

---

4. Therefore, either R or S.

Constructive dilemma is really a combination of modus ponens and disjunctive syllogism. Rather than affirming the antecedent of one conditional, it affirms the disjunction of the antecedents of two conditionals.

As you may suspect, there are many other ways of combining multiple rules of inference in a single argument. We have now examined all six of the main rules of inference used in sentential logic. Naturally, three- and four-step standard forms may not be enough to capture the nuances of an argument. We should therefore pause to demonstrate some different ways of combining them to build a more sophisticated case.

Combinations

A great way to master sentential logic's rules of inference is to read and write newspaper editorials. In the broad sense of the word, a newspaper editorial might take different forms.

- The 'opinion page' of a newspaper typically contains a few short articles by guest writers with special knowledge of their topic.
- 'Letters to the editor' are submitted by ordinary readers, though they are selected and edited by the newspaper staff before publication.
- 'Viewpoint columns' by newspaper staff columnists concern various current events.

What all of these types of editorials have in common is that the author takes a position on an issue and defends it with an argument. Some of the arguments are better than others, of course – ideal fodder for up-and-coming critical thinkers.

Since the dawn of the internet age, blogging has provided another opportunity for editorializing. Most newspapers have websites with blogs. The problem with blogging is that the submissions are so informal and spontaneous that they generally don't bear serious logical evaluation. The old-fashioned editorials, in contrast, are proof-read by someone and wouldn't be published if they weren't carefully considered. They contain interesting arguments while being more accessible than academic or professional writing.

To write an editorial, begin by picking a topic you feel passionately about. Next, state your proposal in one clear sentence. Then list the most important reasons for your proposal. Finally, fill in the logic that connects your reasons to your proposal.

Let's look at the following example.

The topic: Violent crime in Gamerton

The proposal: The mayor should increase police security in Gamerton.

The reasons:

1. There have been seven violent crimes in Gamerton in the past year, the highest crime rate among towns of the same size in the entire country.
2. The alcohol tax that used to pay for extra policing has been diverted to the new prison on the false promise that the prison industry will bring economic prosperity to Gamerton.
3. It is better to prevent crime than to punish criminals because the revenue from the prison goes to just a few bureaucrats while security is enjoyed by everyone.

The logic:

1. Either the alcohol tax should go to the police or it should go to the prison.
2. If the alcohol tax should go to the prison, then the resulting wealth must be shared by all.
3. But the resulting wealth cannot be shared by all.

_____

4. So, the alcohol tax should not go to the prison.

_____

5. Therefore, the alcohol tax should go to the police.

This argument combines two rules of inference: disjunctive syllogism (steps 1, 4, and 5) and modus tollens (steps 2–4).

Now that we have our argument planned out, we can write our letter to the newspaper:

POLICE OR PRISON

The brutal murder of Cassandra Thomas, owner of the corner grocery on Emma Street, is yet another indictment of Gamerton's inadequate police force. Although Gamerton used to be so safe that no one bothered to lock their front doors, criminal activity has been on the rise. Last year there were seven violent crimes, the highest rate among small towns in the entire country.

What's caused this alarming change?

The local alcohol tax used to raise thousands of dollars every year to fund extra police patrolling. When Mayor Batke took office, however, he diverted this revenue to the new prison. As a result, the police force had to cut back on its services.

Many people welcomed the new prison because it promised to bring economic prosperity to Gamerton. But this turns out to be a lie. Most of the employees at the prison make minimum wage and all the profits go straight into the pockets of a few fat cat bureaucrats.

This week, the mayor proposed a multi-million-dollar expansion of the original prison plan. We must stop this madness and give the alcohol tax back to the police force. Security is a precious resource, enjoyed equally by all.

Notice we added some interesting details that didn't appear in the standard form and we did not spell out the steps of our reasoning. Nevertheless, the letter benefited from the careful thought we put into its logical structure.

People who submit editorials to the newspaper probably don't often write out their arguments in standard form. Nevertheless, if they are effective writers, then the same logic is implicitly guiding their thought process.

To see this, let's read the following editorial and reconstruct the logic behind it.

LIE DETECTOR TESTS LIE

The lie detector test, also known as the 'polygraph', is a great device for Hollywood justice. Like Wonder Woman's golden lasso, the polygraph promises to trap evil-doers into helpless confessions. This fantasy couldn't be further from the truth.

The polygraph works on the assumption that human beings undergo uncontrollable physiological changes when they lie. It measures and records responses in the subject's blood pressure, pulse, respiration, and skin conductivity while an interviewer asks a series of questions.

The problem is that good liars can learn how to control their physiological responses. This has been documented in a number of famous espionage cases, including the case of double-agent Aldrich Ames, who passed two polygraph tests while spying for the Soviet Union. When asked how he did it, he replied that he simply got a good night's sleep, cultivated a friendly rapport with the interviewer, and relaxed.

Dawn Rummy is a key witness in the Cassandra Thomas murder case who claims she saw Mark Deal pull the trigger. She recently passed a lie detector test. But Ms Rummy is also a teenaged substance abuser. This is a category of person known to be highly practiced in the art of deception. It is an outrage that the presiding judge would admit her lie detector test as evidence in a court of law.

Notice this letter does not use a single conditional statement. Nevertheless, the 'assumption' mentioned at the beginning of the second paragraph introduces the same logical leverage as a conditional statement. This suggests we begin our standard form as follows:

1. If the lie detector test is a reliable form of evidence, then all human beings undergo uncontrollable physiological changes when they lie.

2. But it is not the case that all human beings undergo uncontrollable physiological changes when they lie.

---

3. So, the lie detector test is not a reliable form of evidence.

We used 'So' in step 3 because it is clearly not the end of the argument. The author's main conclusion is that the judge should not admit the lie detector test. We can get there by adding one more step:

4. If the lie detector test is not a reliable form of evidence, then it should not be admitted in the Cassandra Thomas murder case.

---

5. Therefore, the lie detector test should not be admitted in the Cassandra Thomas murder case.

This five-step standard form combines modus tollens and modus ponens. The subconclusion of the modus tollens argument at step 3 serves as the first premise of the modus ponens argument, affirming the antecedent of the conditional statement at step 4. (Recall that the conditional statement does not have to come first.) There may be other ways to represent the thought behind the editorial but this is a legitimate interpretation and it puts us in a good position to evaluate it.

Sometimes newspapers print letters responding to editorials. We could write up a criticism of the above editorial as follows:

ABSURD STANDARDS

I read the editorial 'Lie detector tests lie' in astonishment. The author clearly does not understand the wisdom in the ancient principle 'the exception proves the rule'. The double-agent Aldrich Ames is famous precisely because he is an extremely rare individual.

The aspect of human physiology that controls emotional response is called the 'sympathetic nervous system'. When the

ABSURD STANDARDS (*cont.*)

sympathetic nervous system functions correctly, it is completely involuntary. If Mr. Ames could control his blood pressure and pulse, then his sympathetic nervous system was probably malfunctioning. It is far more likely that Mr. Ames suffered from a physiological impairment than that he was well practiced in the art of deception.

There are always anomalies. To say that, in order to be reliable, the lie detector test has to work for all human beings is to say it has to be 100 percent accurate. And to say that it has to be 100% accurate is to say that any test admitted in a court of law has to be 100 percent accurate. But this is absurd. The best physicians use far less accurate tests to make life or death decisions about their patients.

For example, DNA tests are used to detect cancer. The newest, most accurate one available is still only 95 percent accurate. Yet I guarantee you that doctors will be more than happy to use that test as evidence for making diagnoses that result in treatments and surgeries with irreversible consequences.

Nothing in life is 100 percent. That's why the exception proves the rule.

The author of this response is attacking premise 1 of the above standard form, according to which the lie detector test needs to work for all human beings in order to be a reliable form of evidence.

Notice how the author undermines this claim in order to conclude the opposite. We can represent the argument in standard form as follows.

To prove: the lie detector test does not need to work for all human beings in order to be admitted in a court of law.

1. Suppose the lie detector test needed to work for all human beings in order to be admitted in a court of law.
2. If the lie detector test needed to work for all human beings in order to be admitted in a court of law, then it must be 100 percent accurate to count as evidence.

3. If the lie detector test must be 100 percent accurate to count as evidence, then any test must be 100% accurate to count as evidence.
4. If any test must be 100 percent accurate to count as evidence, then DNA tests must be 100% accurate to count as evidence.

---

5. So, if the lie detector test needed to work for all human beings in order to be admitted in a court of law, then DNA tests must be 100 percent accurate to count as evidence.
6. But it is absurd to suppose DNA tests must be 100 percent accurate to count as evidence since they don't even need to be 95 percent accurate in order to diagnose cancer.

---

7. Therefore, the lie detector test does not need to work for all human beings in order to be admitted in a court of law.

This argument combines two of the rules of inference we learned in this chapter: while the framework follows the reductio ad absurdum format, the conditional step in the middle is iterated three times in accordance with hypothetical syllogism.

We could fabricate many more examples of many more combinations. For example:
Disjunctive syllogism and modus ponens:

1. Either P or Q.
2. Not-Q.

---

3. So, P.
4. If P, then R.

---

5. Therefore, R.

Hypothetical syllogism with multiple iteration, and modus ponens:

1. If P, then Q.

2. If Q, then R.
3. If R, then S.
4. If S, then T.

_____

5. So, if P, then T.
6. P.

_____

7. Therefore, T.

Constructive dilemma with disjunctive syllogism and modus tollens:

1. Either P or Q.
2. If P, then R.
3. If Q, then S.

_____

4. So, either R or S.
5. Not-R

_____

6. So, S.
7. If T, then not-S.

_____

8. Therefore, not-T.

The possibilities are endless! But there is no need to get carried away. Most real arguments can be captured in just a few steps. Let's look at some examples for you to try.

Exercises

Reconstruct the arguments in the following newspaper editorial excerpts, looking for instances of the rules of inference examined in this chapter. As with the exercises in the previous chapters, begin by drawing a blank standard form and then filling in the conclusion first. The conclusion is the main thing the author is trying to prove. Bear in mind that you will need to supply unmentioned steps and eliminate irrelevancies. Scribble a number of different possibilities on scrap paper until you capture the logic accurately. There is always more than one way to do it correctly. Identify the rule or rules of inference you use. Compare your answers to the key at the back of this book.

Trade pact saps manufacturing jobs

If NAFTA were really a free trade agreement, it would contain just a page or two on eliminating tariffs.

Instead, NAFTA is an 824-page tome packed with rules to protect drug companies, banks and Wall Street investors. Safeguards for workers, the environment or food quality don't merit even a footnote.

Sherod Brown, *USA Today*, Friday 29 February 2008, p.8A

Act now to save the salmon

As global warming bears down on our Western rivers and watersheds, it threatens one of the great symbols of Western abundance: wild salmon. With each passing year, their numbers have dropped precipitously. This decline is believed to be in part the result of warming temperatures in streams and rivers.

Just last week, government fishery managers moved toward a ban on salmon fishing off the California and Oregon coasts because of the diminishing numbers of Chinook salmon.

If we hope to save the salmon, we must do two things: stop the rise in greenhouse gases as quickly as we can and secure our waters' health against the warming that has begun and will continue. This is a river-by-river job and each river matters.

Carl Pope, *Los Angeles Times*,
Friday 21 March 2008, p. A19

Bonus baby

J. Kenneth Blackwell's successor as secretary of state, Democrat Jennifer Brunner, was the one who blew the whistle. But it's Blackwell's fellow Republican, State Auditor Mary Taylor, who is assessing the penalty.

Taylor, following up on a request last year from the newly arrived Brunner for an audit of the secretary of state's office, found that Blackwell paid $80,534 in going-away bonuses to the members of his staff . . .

Taylor's audit also found that Blackwell left without leaving Brunner an inventory of property and assets of the office. That wasn't merely discourteous; it was illegal.

Presumably, Brunner and her staff have located all of the staplers and three-hole punches by now, but such lapses certainly don't promote orderly transitions in government. If Blackwell's failure to provide his successor the most complete rundown of the administrative state of the office was an innocent oversight, it bespeaks a lack of seriousness. If it was done consciously, it bespeaks pettiness unworthy of a public servant in state office.

The Plain Dealer, Thursday, March 27, 2008, p. B6

Closing the achievement gap

If we do nothing, statewide budget cuts will deepen the inequities that already exist among students in the Pasadena Unified School District.

So, we must do something.

That's why several different community organizations are getting together Saturday at All Saints Church to host a community summit on what must be done. The aim is to involve not only schools administrators and elected officials in helping our kids, but also teachers, parents and other concerned members of the community who can help offer real solutions.

Raúl Borbón and Susana Zamorano, *Pasadena Weekly*,
Thursday 13 March 2008, p. 10

The *Nature* editorial

The editors [of *Nature* magazine] assert that the emergence of the human mind without intelligent design is an 'unassailable fact'. Perhaps the most remarkable thing about this claim, aside from the problems with their interpretation of the scientific evidence itself, is the admission by the editors that the question of intelligent design in biology can be adjudicated by the scientific method. If the evidence for or against intelligent design can be evaluated scientifically – as the editors at *Nature* firmly assert that it can – then intelligent design is a real scientific inference, albeit, according to the *Nature* editors, a mistaken one. And if they are asserting that intelligent design is mistaken from a non-scientific standpoint, then the editors are advancing an atheistic theology, as Brownback pointed out.

The mainstay of the materialists' argument against intelligent design has been that it isn't science. Yet, as the *Nature* editors inadvertently demonstrate so clearly, the materialists' argument against intelligent design is self-refuting; they argue that intelligent design isn't science, and that it's scientifically wrong. Yet if intelligent design is scientifically wrong – if it is an 'unassailable fact' that the human mind is the product of evolution, not intelligent design – then the design inference can be investigated (and, they claim, refuted) using the scientific method. Then intelligent design is science.

Either the conclusion that the editors reached is the result of a scientific analysis of the design inference, or the conclusion that the editors reached is the result of a non-scientific analysis of the design inference, which would be, as Senator Brownback observed, atheistic theology posing as science.

Either intelligent design is science, or Senator Brownback got it right.

> Michael Egnor, *The Discovery Institute: Evolution News and Views*, 18 June 2007

No retreat from the War on Terror

In recent days, and unsurprisingly, it has become common to hear the mournless rites being read for liberal interventionism. If anyone has opined publicly about Afghanistan in the last week – and plenty did – it was to regret our presence there and to wish us away. If ever an argument was being won by default this was it, especially since those making the case for quitting were far too exuberant to want to slow up and allow for the possible objections to their reasoning . . .

Canada has already threatened to pull out its troops from Kandahar province in a year's time if other NATO countries don't contribute more. We must assume that if Britain were to begin to talk about a draw-down, then Canada would carry out this threat. British forces would then be exposed in Helmand and, presumably, would also withdraw. Let us suppose that an angry and abandoned US follows the 'lead' offered by its allies, and itself pulls out, leaving itself only an air-to-ground interdiction capability.

Here are the likely consequences of such a pattern. The Afghan Government would collapse, to be replaced by an overt civil war fought between the Taleban and local governors in the various provinces. A million or more Afghan refugees would again flee their country, many of them ending up in the West. Deprived of support from the US, as recommended by our commentators, President Musharraf or a successor would effectively withdraw from the border regions, leaving a vast lawless area from central Afghanistan to north central Pakistan. Al-Qaeda and other jihadists would operate from these areas as they did before 9/11. This time these forces – already capable of assassinating a popular democratic politician – would seriously impact upon the stability of Pakistan, which is a nuclear state.

Jihadists everywhere, from Indonesia to Palestine, would see this as a huge victory, democrats and moderates as a catastrophic defeat. There would hardly be a country, from Morocco to Malaysia, that wouldn't feel the impact of the reverse. That's before we calculate the cost to women and girls of no longer being educated or allowed medical treatment.

David Aaronovitch, *The London Times*, 5 February 2008

Why Israel must kvetch

Listen to Prime Minister Ehud Olmert after his country suffered through months of bombings, including the recent brutal murder of Jewish students in Jerusalem: 'Despite terrorism and despite the pain, we are not relinquishing the monumental task of making another dramatic step that can bring us closer to building the foundations for true peace between Israel and the Palestinians.'

Those are the words of a taskmaster, not a PR meister.

What creates good PR is pessimism, not optimism – being offended, not accommodating. Smart PR is geared to the people who spend nanoseconds thinking about your cause, which is about 99 percent of the planet. Those people don't look at your body of facts; they look at your body language.

When your body language shows no emotion, when you don't even react to being stabbed in the back, you look guilty. In the Middle East, the way to fight the PR battle is not to stay calm, but to show more outrage than your enemy.

If defending Israel's image was a priority for Olmert, he would regularly criticize the behaviour of his 'peace partner' Abbas, who continues to preside over the indoctrination of hate in Palestinian society, and who, while pretending to be a peace-maker, praises terrorists and reiterates his refusal to recognize Israel when speaking to the Arab press.

But unlike Abbas, Olmert doesn't kvetch about his adversaries. In fact, our formidable Mount Rushmore of stone-faced leaders – Olmert, Peres, Barak, and Livni – will kvetch a lot less about the murder of Jews than the Palestinians will wail about Israeli housing permits in Gush Etzion. That's why they cream us in PR. They're always wailing.

David Suissa, *Jewish Journal*, 14 March 2008, p. 4

4

Informal argument evaluation

In a heated argument we are apt to lose sight of the truth.

Publilius Syrus

Standard form reconstruction enables you to launch a formal evaluation of an argument. This is especially helpful in a written context, such as a paper, an article, or a letter, where you can identify and organize the steps of reasoning. Formal evaluation involves checking for fallacies. We have already learned the seven most important formal fallacies: in chapter 2, the five syllogistic fallacies; in chapter 3, the fallacy of affirming the consequent and the fallacy of denying the antecedent. All of these errors are known as 'formal fallacies' because they destroy the deductive validity of the argument, leaving the author without a logical line of reasoning.

Arguments can also be evaluated in an informal manner. You can detect informal fallacies without even reconstructing the argument in standard form. While the formal fallacies commit errors that are objectively demonstrable, the informal fallacies are subjective, meaning there is no way to prove or disprove them. Those who commit informal fallacies are using problematic reasons that undermine the strength of their arguments. Nevertheless, they can always defend themselves based on considerations of context or purpose. So it is up to each critical thinker to decide for him- or herself whether or not a given instance is genuinely objectionable or not. Although you cannot prove informal fallacies, identifying possible instances of them, both in your own arguments and in the arguments of others, will enable you to think more clearly about any issue.

In this chapter, we will look at the fifteen most common and most damaging informal fallacies, which can be divided into three categories: relevance, presumption, and ambiguity.

Informal fallacies are rare in academic and professional writing because this work is written, revised, and edited with so much care that by the time it's published, any obvious problems have been removed. You are more likely to run into the informal fallacies in blogs and editorials, which are less carefully prepared. But you are most likely to run into them in spoken conversation, when people are presenting arguments spontaneously. On such occasions, emotions cloud our judgment and make it difficult to concentrate on good reasons for or against the proposal under consideration. For the purpose of studying the fifteen informal fallacies, therefore, let's pretend we're flies on the wall at a meeting of three detectives working on the Cassandra Thomas murder case.

WHO'S GUILTY?

The characters

Detective Steven Piper: Senior homicide detective, Gamerton Police Department

Detective Henry Sheldon: Private investigator, hired by the father of Dawn Rummy, a teenage girl who claims to have witnessed Mark Deal shoot Cassandra Thomas.

Detective Kimberly Binchy: Private investigator, hired by Mark Deal, who claims he was in Moscow at the time of the murder.

The setting

A sparse, windowless room at Police Headquarters

Five fallacies of relevance

The first five fallacies are called 'fallacies of relevance' because they advance reasons that should not have any bearing on the issue.

Hello, Kim and Henry. Thanks for meeting with me today. Perhaps we can make better progress on this case by pooling our information. We have a common goal after all: to find out the truth.

Steve, everyone knows Mark Deal is guilty. Why don't you just haul him in here and get a confession out of him?

1. Ad populum: the fallacy of claiming that popularity establishes truth

Henry commits the fallacy ad populum when he argues that everyone knows Mark Deal is guilty. Ad populum is often used in advertisements, as in 'Everyone loves Pepsi!' It also may be familiar to you from your own childhood, as in 'Please, Mom, everyone's doing it!'

Popularity is a problematic argument strategy for two main reasons. First of all, it's almost always false. If everyone were already on board with the proposal, then there wouldn't be any need to make the argument in the first place. Secondly, it's manipulative. Human beings have a natural instinct to want to fit in, to be part of the crowd. This is why ad populum is sometimes called the 'band wagon' fallacy. It implies that if you don't agree, you're going to be left off the band wagon, alone in the cold. But this shouldn't be a consideration in serious discussions. History gives countless examples of brave men and women who were willing to contradict popular opinion for the sake of the truth. Consider Galileo, who dared to assert that the Earth is not the centre of the Universe at a time when nearly everyone, including religious authorities, insisted that it was. Civilization would never progress if we allowed popularity to decide the issues.

2. Ad ignorantiam: the fallacy of supposing lack of proof proves something

Kim commits the fallacy ad ignorantiam when she insists that Cassandra is no mobster because she was never proven to be one. True, in the legal system we must treat people as innocent unless proven guilty. But Kim seems to think Cassandra really is innocent because her accusers were not able to find proof of guilt.

Lack of proof never proves anything. Just because we have so far failed to find evidence for a claim doesn't mean the claim isn't true. Conversely, just because we have so far failed to find evidence *against* a claim doesn't mean it isn't false. If you go looking for evidence for or against a claim and fail to find it, the only thing you are entitled to conclude is that the claim is unproven.

In ancient times, most people believed the Earth is flat.

Although some intellectuals were convinced the Earth is round, there was no way to prove it. This didn't prove they were wrong! On the contrary, we eventually proved they were right. In other cases, human beings may never find proof one way or the other. When we lack proof we advance theories and limit our conclusions to the available evidence.

Regardless of what happened ten years ago, we now know Cassandra is the leader of a thriving drug ring.

But that's impossible. I interviewed the coroner who performed her autopsy. He said her shop is on the brink of bankruptcy and she could barely pay her rent.

3. Ad verecundiam: the fallacy of relying on an inappropriate authority

There are many times when it is appropriate to appeal to authority in an argument. For 'example, if you were debating whether or not to have a picnic, the weather forecaster's prediction of rain would be highly relevant. However, there are at least three instances in which use of authority in an argument is fallacious.

In the first instance, an authority in one field might be used in another, unrelated field. Henry makes this mistake when he cites the coroner as an authority on Cassandra's finances.

In the second instance, someone might be treated as an authority even though they have no special qualifications at all. For example, people often take medical advice from friends and family members, as in 'My cousin says smoking isn't so bad as long as you use filters'.

In the third instance, tradition might be treated as an authority.

While tradition may often give us a clue to tried and true practices, it is often without justification. After all, slavery was a tradition.

So, when using authority in an argument, critical thinkers need to beware of irrelevant authorities, unqualified authorities, and unjustified traditions.

At any rate, we have established that Cassandra was selling mafia drugs to Dawn when she was shot..

Well, then, we better bury this case fast. Do you think the mafia is going to let us live to reveal the truth? They're probably waiting outside right now . . .

More likely, they're probably after poor little Dawn. For God's sake, Steve, get a quick confession out of Mark and put Dawn in witness protection!

4. Red herring: the fallacy of changing the subject

Years ago, when hunters used dogs to chase game through the wilderness, they needed something to help them call the dogs off when the time came. They used a smoked fish called 'red herring'. When the hunters brought out the fish, its strong scent attracted the dogs and made them forget about what they were chasing.

People sometimes make a similar move in the midst of an argument. They sense the opponent moving in for the kill and they don't have a good counterargument, so they raise a different issue, hoping to be able to distract the opponent from a successful conclusion. Such distraction can also occur by accident if someone who is not fully focused on the issue raises an irrelevant point that sidetracks the argument.

Although there are unlimited ways to commit the red herring fallacy, two are especially common.

The first, called 'ad baculum', is an appeal to force or threats. Kim commits this fallacy when she argues that, if they don't bury the case fast, the mafia will come after them. The second most common form of red herring, called 'ad misericordiam', is an appeal to pity or guilt. Henry commits this form of the fallacy when he tries to convince Steve to arrest Mark in order to save Dawn.

5. Ad hominem: the fallacy of attacking the person instead of the argument

Argumentation is very demanding. When people become tired, frustrated, or upset, they may resort to low blows. Politicians call this 'mudslinging'. Logicians call it 'ad hominem', which means 'against the person'. There are four main forms to watch for.

Circumstantial ad hominem occurs when someone claims the opponent is biased due to his or her circumstances. Kim commits this form of the fallacy when she accuses Henry of blaming Mark because Dawn's father is paying him a mint. It may be that Henry has a vested interest in casting Mark as the murderer, but this doesn't prove Mark is innocent.

Abusive ad hominem occurs when someone insults or belittles the opponent in an effort to win the argument. Henry commits this form of the fallacy when he says Mark charmed Kim's skirt off. This comment is offensively sexist and it implies that Kim is conducting herself unprofessionally.

Poisoning the well is a form of ad hominem also known as 'guilt by association'. In this case, someone tries to refute the opponent by connecting him or her to something undesirable. For example, to say someone's proposal 'sounds like Nazi propaganda' would be to project the negative judgment most people have about Nazis onto the proposal.

Finally, the form of ad hominem known as 'tu quoque' means 'you did it too'. This is where someone accuses the opponent of hypocrisy. For example, suppose Henry accuses Kim of hiding evidence against Mark. It would be an instance of the tu quoque fallacy for Kim to accuse Henry of doing the same thing for Dawn. Kim needs to refute Henry's accusation before launching one of her own. Two wrongs don't make a right.

Notice that any of the forms of ad hominem can also be considered red herrings in so far as they function to change the subject.

Five fallacies of presumption

The next five fallacies are called 'fallacies of presumption' because the reasoning involved proceeds by assuming the truth of a claim that is either false or uncertain.

Hello, Kim and Henry. Thanks for coming back. As you may recall, Dawn swears she saw Mark shoot Cassandra. We learned last time, however, that Dawn was buying drugs from Cassandra at the time of the shooting and that she had a prior relationship with Mark. These two factors give us reason to question her testimony.

But Dawn passed a lie detector test!

That test was clearly faulty. Dawn's a drug addict. All addicts are liars and they will lie about anything. Didn't you see the news story last week about the guy caught lying repeatedly to his doctor about an injury in order to get Vicodin?

1. Hasty generalization: the fallacy of inferring from some to all

Hasty generalization occurs when one presumes too quickly that there are no significant differences among the members of a group. Kim makes a doubly hasty generalization when she says, 'All addicts are liars and they will lie about anything'. As evidence for this claim she cites just one addict who lied about just one thing.

Most judgments depend on some degree of generalization. Consider the simple statement 'I like movies'. Surely not even the most avid movie fan likes every movie ever made. It's understood that general claims admit of exceptions.

But generalizing can be dangerous, as is evident in the case of stereotyping. Someone who had problems with a few members of a particular group may be tempted to infer that all members of this group cause problems. This judgment is inaccurate and unfair since the members of any given group may be quite different from one another. Racism and sexism involve entrenched stereotypes derived from hasty generalizations.

2. Begging the question: the fallacy of circular reasoning

In this exchange, Steve asks whether Dawn might have shot Cassandra. In so doing, he indicates he thinks Dawn might be a violent person. Henry argues Dawn couldn't have shot Cassandra because she's not violent. But how does Henry know whether or not Dawn is violent? Whether or not Dawn is violent depends on whether or not she shot Cassandra. So, Henry is arguing in a circle: Dawn didn't shoot Cassandra because she's not violent and she's not violent because she didn't shoot Cassandra.

Henry shouldn't use the claim that Dawn is not violent as a reason for his conclusion that she didn't shoot Cassandra because this is the very claim Steve is doubting. A good argument starts from premises the opponent may be willing to accept and shows how those very premises lead to your conclusion. If the opponent accepts the premises, then he or she must accept your conclusion.

You can tell an argument begs the question when the reason given for the conclusion is really just another way of saying the same thing as the conclusion. The opponent needs to be given a reason different from the conclusion in order to be persuaded.

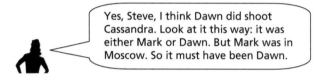

Yes, Steve, I think Dawn did shoot Cassandra. Look at it this way: it was either Mark or Dawn. But Mark was in Moscow. So it must have been Dawn.

3. False dilemma: the fallacy of reducing a variety of options to just two

Whenever someone tells you that you have a choice between just two options, you should always ask yourself whether more possibilities have been left out. In the last chapter, we examined the rule of inference known as disjunctive syllogism:

1. P or Q.
2. Not-Q.
   _____

3. Therefore, P.

Although this is a deductively valid argument, the first premise is vulnerable. Are there really just two options? An opponent may object that the argument commits the fallacy of false dilemma.

Kim makes this mistake when she assumes the killer was either Mark or Dawn. Why are they the only two possibilities? False dilemma is a fallacy of presumption because it illegitimately assumes that all the other possibilities have been eliminated.

4. Post hoc (false cause): the fallacy of assuming that x caused y simply because x preceded y.

The term 'post hoc' is Latin shorthand for *post hoc ergo propter hoc*, which means 'after this therefore because of this'.

Steve may be committing the post hoc fallacy when he suggests that Dawn's father, Boxer, caused his computer to crash. Just because Steve's computer crashed after Boxer was there doesn't mean Boxer did it. On the other hand, it is possible that he did.

In order to determine whether or not someone is committing the post hoc fallacy, we need to ask two questions.

1. Is there a plausible explanation for how and why x caused y?

Some people believe wearing a charm bracelet to a football game can help their team win. This is a clear case of the post hoc fallacy because there is no plausible way to explain how or why a bracelet could improve a team's performance. If the team wins when the bracelet is present, it will be a coincidence and the belief in a connection will be nothing but superstition.

If Steve can explain how and why Boxer made his computer crash then we wouldn't accuse him of committing the post hoc fallacy. But there is another important question to ask.

2. Is there a common cause of both x and y?

Suppose your car refuses to start every time you find the cat in the garage. You may be inclined to conclude the cat is somehow causing the malfunction. However, cold, damp weather may be the common cause of the behavior of both the car and the cat. In this case, we would say their behavior is correlated by a common cause.

Likewise, suppose Boxer went to the police station because someone crashed *his* computer. Then it might be reasonable to suspect that whoever crashed Boxer's computer also crashed Steve's. This person would be the common cause of the correlation.

5. Straw man: the fallacy of oversimplifying the opponent's view to make it easy to refute

It can be very difficult to refute an opponent's argument, which may be long, complex, and full of compelling points. As a critical thinker, you have to find a way to deflate it while at the same time taking it seriously.

'Straw man' is an old-fashioned word for a scarecrow. Needless to say, it's easy to knock down a straw man – even a child can do it.

Refuting an opponent's view by oversimplifying it is like knocking down a straw man. By replacing the real target with a fake one, you fail to accomplish your task and leave the impression you're not up to it.

Henry commits the straw man fallacy when he accuses Steve of 'basically saying' Boxer is stupid. Steve wasn't saying that at all; he was actually imputing a very clever strategy to Boxer. Watch carefully any time someone uses the phrase 'You're basically saying . . .' because nine times out of ten an oversimplification is forthcoming.

The way to avoid straw man is to practice what logicians call the 'principle of charity': always interpret your opponent's view in the best possible light. If you give your opponents their due then your arguments will be more meaningful. Think of it this way: martial arts practitioners always bow to one another before they pounce. They would never want to make false presumptions about the weakness of their opponent.

Five fallacies of ambiguity

The remaining five fallacies are called 'fallacies of ambiguity' because they arise due to confusion over the meaning of words.

1. Is-ought: the fallacy of inferring a prescriptive statement from a descriptive statement

In the last chapter we saw that descriptive statements assert facts while prescriptive statements assert values. Because of this difference, it is a fallacy to infer prescriptive statements from descriptive statements.

Kim probably commits the is–ought fallacy when she suggests Henry should stop defending his client because he's dead. Her argument could be reconstructed as follows:

1. Boxer is a dead client.
2. You should not defend dead clients.

---

3. You should not defend Boxer.

Of course, we can't be critical of Kim for neglecting to spell out her argument in standard form, since this not expected in spoken arguments. Moreover, the standard form is valid. So, what's the problem?

The problem is it's not clear Kim understands she's making a value judgment. She seems to think that the fact of death automatically releases people from their obligations in the same way that the fact of death automatically causes decay. But release from an obligation is not like decay. As a physical process, decay is a fact. This is why it can be caused by death: facts can cause facts. Release from an obligation is not a physical process. It's a value judgment. While facts can *influence* value judgments, they cannot automatically cause them.

In most instances of the is–ought fallacy, the speaker doesn't even realize he or she is inferring a value from a fact. This is why the is–ought fallacy can be considered a fallacy of ambiguity.

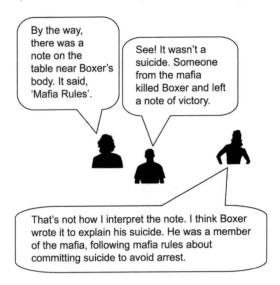

2. Amphiboly: the fallacy of creating two meanings through faulty sentence structure

A great number of arguments arise through misunderstanding. In fact, when opponents take time to express themselves clearly, they often find they have nothing to argue about.

Critical thinkers strive to write and speak as clearly as possible to avoid wasting time over nonexistent disagreements.

Nevertheless, in the heat of the moment, we sometime fail to construct careful sentences. The result is amphiboly.

Sometimes amphiboly arises through abbreviated language. The note Steve found at the crime scene, 'Mafia Rules', is amphibolous because it could mean two different things. While there are no errors in it, it does not provide enough information for a reliable interpretation.

Other times, amphiboly arises through grammatical errors. Suppose Henry and Kim demand a handwriting analysis of the note in order to determine its author and Steve responds:

We have equipment to check the handwriting on the table.

According to this sentence, someone has written on the table. What Steve should have said was:

We have equipment on the table to check the handwriting.

It is often left to the listener to pay careful attention to the context of sentences in order to avoid interpreting them in the wrong way.

Kim's interpretation of the note can't be correct. The mafia is a rich, Italian organization. Boxer was neither rich nor Italian. Besides, Boxer was a really nice guy. If the mafia made him a member, then I'd say we don't need to worry about the mafia any more.

3 and 4. Distribution: the fallacies of inferring from the whole to a part (division) or from a part to the whole (composition)

If you see an angry mob on the street is it safe to assume that each individual in the group is angry? Perhaps. If you are served a terrible dinner at a restaurant, are you justified in never going back? Perhaps. In each of these cases you're making a distribution inference. In the first case, you're inferring from the whole to a part; in the second, you're inferring from a part to the whole. Distribution inferences are common and generally harmless because parts and wholes very often share the same qualities.

Nevertheless, there are some cases in which distribution will lead you astray. Henry commits the fallacy of division when he denies Boxer could be a member of the mafia because it is a rich, Italian organization while Boxer is neither rich nor Italian. An organization is liable to have qualities that are lacking in individual members. The reverse is true as well, as we see when Henry asserts that, if the mafia did hire Boxer, then it must be a harmless organization. He reasons that, if one member of the mafia is harmless, then the entire mafia must be harmless. This is the fallacy of composition. A large group can admit a great deal of variation in its members without changing the identity of the group itself.

The same point applies to objects as well. Just because a car can go speeding down the highway doesn't mean its dashboard can. And just because the dashboard of a car is ugly doesn't mean the whole car is.

The fallacies of distribution can be considered instances of ambiguity because they arise from the confusion of thinking that a part is a microcosm of the whole.

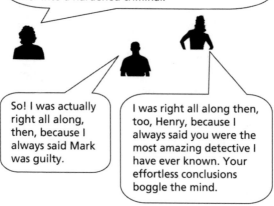

Well, I'm afraid you're both wrong. We caught Dawn fleeing the scene. She confessed to the murder of both Cassandra and her father. She killed Cassandra for drugs and then she killed her father to prevent him from turning her in. She claims the year she spent with Mark turned her into a hardened criminal.

So! I was actually right all along, then, because I always said Mark was guilty.

I was right all along then, too, Henry, because I always said you were the most amazing detective I have ever known. Your effortless conclusions boggle the mind.

5. Equivocation: the fallacy of using the same word in two different ways

Critical thinkers spend a good deal of time defining their terms. Otherwise, as in the case of amphiboly, a phantom disagreement may emerge.

For example, 'freedom' can refer to the ability to choose one's own destiny or to political rights. Someone who thinks we're free in one sense may not think we're free in the other sense. So it would be futile to embark on a discussion of freedom without making clear which kind is at stake. If you change from one meaning to the other midstream, you commit the fallacy of equivocation.

The fallacy of equivocation is often used as a last ditch effort to twist the terms of the discussion around to make it appear that you've won. Henry claims he was right all along because he knew Mark was guilty. But here he uses the word 'guilty' in a very different sense than he did at the beginning. At the beginning he meant Mark was guilty of shooting Cassandra. Now he means Mark is guilty of corrupting Dawn. This is a big difference. The first kind of guilt is illegal, the second kind isn't.

Kim's final backhanded compliment to Henry is also a case of equivocation. The word 'effortless' has two completely different meanings, one positive, one negative. Likewise, the words 'amazing' and 'boggle the mind' change meaning depending on how we interpret 'effortless'. Understanding Kim's comment hinges on seeing how Henry is invited to interpret it one way, while we interpret it the other way. Of course, we wouldn't accuse Kim of committing a fallacy here since she is deliberately making a joke.

The end

Hopefully, this story provides examples that will help you to remember the informal fallacies when you encounter them in your daily life. It will also help to practice identifying fallacies, as in the following exercises.

Exercises

Identify possible instances of informal fallacies in the following editorial excerpts. How might the authors defend themselves against your charge? How might you revise their arguments to avoid concerns about fallacious reasoning? Check your answers against the key at the back of this book.

History lesson

Perhaps Scott Rowed doesn't know that the U.S. Supreme Court twice – in 1964 and 1969 – defined humanism as a religion. So whose religion will deal with education – mine or his?

According to him we should have no choice. That is the height of arrogance and ignorance combined.

Rowed is zealous in furthering the agenda of the Frankfurt School (headed by such socialist 'thinkers' as Marcuse, Lukacz, Gramsci and others) with its 'critical theory,' where everything Christian is rendered fit for attack.

As for separation of church and state, why is his religion of humanistic dogmatism not separated from the state; why does this principle only apply to Christianity? This is simply intolerance masquerading as tolerance.

Our whole educational system originated in the Catholic Church. It was Pope Innocent IV who, in 1254, granted the privilege of awarding degrees to the Oxford University.

Fr. John Sembrat, *The Edmonton Journal*,
Monday 24 March 2008, p. a9

If not now, when?

We all know that Ohio is in economic trouble. We have been struggling to keep our bright, young adults here after graduation. Our elected officials are working overtime to keep jobs in this area and to attract new companies to make this their base of operation. Akron's mayor and our Summit County executive have made economic development a top priority.

One key to achieving these goals is to pass the Equal Housing and Employment Act (EHEA), which was introduced last week in both the Ohio House and Senate. This bill would ban discrimination based on sexual orientation and gender identity.

Polls indicate that young professionals favour locating in cities that are welcoming to diversity. Many successful corporations have adopted non-discrimination policies, knowing they must do this to attract the best of the new talent. These companies are looking for locations that support those policies.

In addition, the electorate in Ohio and nationally has indicated that it is ready for such legislation, with 66 percent of Ohioans saying that they would support a ban on housing and employment discrimination.

At present, 20 states and the District of Columbia ban discrimination on the basis of sexual orientation. Fifteen Ohio cities also support this. The sad truth is that with those 15 Ohio cities, only one-fifth of the population is protected.

Now we in Akron and Ohio have the chance to provide that same protection to the other four-fifths.

Let's help end this senseless discrimination. Let's help Ohio rise to its former economic greatness. Let's be part of the solution by calling our legislators to voice our support for the Equal Housing and Employment Act.

Ingrid C. Kunstel, *Akron Beacon Journal*,
Tuesday 18 March 2008, p. A8

Heather Mills: a greedy woman hits the divorce jackpot

It was in one of those dreary 'Have Your Say' postings that now dot every major news story online and draw the nutters as surely as steaming cow patties do flies that I saw the whinge: 'Why is everyone so hard on her?'

She is Heather Mills, Sir Paul McCartney's estranged wife, who this week got absolutely pummelled by a British judge who, in that excruciatingly even-handed and flawlessly polite

English way, all but called her a lying piggy as he awarded her $48.6 million (U.S.) – only a fraction of the $250 million she had demanded from the couple's divorce settlement . . .

Although she strongly denied it, her case boils down to the syndrome of 'Me too' or, 'If he has it, I want it too'. So, I don't know why the 'everyone' referred to in that posting is hard on Ms Mills, but it's sure why I'm hard on her: This is a greedy woman, who at the ripe old age of 40, after a marriage that lasted all of four years, decided that she should not have to work ever again (not, to be frank, that modelling and 'TV presenting', as the Brits call TV hosting or news reading, is by most measures real work anyway) and who went after the ex with that special viciousness forged in the bedroom.

Christie Blatchford, *Toronto Globe and Mail*,
Saturday 22 March 2008

Global warming, or global con?

The fourth and final assessment of the Intergovernmental Panel on Climate Change reads like the Bible, but gospel it is not.

It is a 'consensus' in that it started with a foregone conclusion – that man-made pollution is dooming the planet – and gathered in any and all opinions that supported it . . .

Our growing world needs more energy, not less. To even keep per capita emissions the same, much less reduce them, would mean freezing everybody's living standards and condemning the world's poor to permanent poverty.

And for what?

Accepting something like Kyoto, which would dismantle our thriving free-market economy while reducing global temperatures by an estimated 0.04 degree Celsius over the next century, an amount too small to measure.

It would achieve this trifling result only at the cost of literally trillions of dollars over that time – money that will not come from some imaginary place or 'global resources', but out of your pocket.

After all, when the U.N. grandly says 'we must work together', what it's really saying is, 'Americans must foot the bill'.

The U.N. would do better to support things like the indoor spraying of DDT in the Third World to fight the rampant malaria that kills millions or bio-engineered crops that promote health while fighting hunger and famine, and oppose things that suppress the economic growth the world needs.

Investor's Business Daily, Monday 19 November 2007

Nader jumps into the Presidential race

Attorney and consumer advocate Ralph Nader, who contested the 2000 Presidential election as a Green Party candidate, announced Sunday that he will attempt to win the White House this year as an Independent.

Appearing on NBC News program 'Meet the Press', Nader said, 'After careful thought and my desire to retire our supremely selected president, I've decided to run as an Independent candidate for president'.

Running as a Green Party presidential candidate in 2000, Nader was accused of tipping the balance away from Al Gore, which helped elect George W. Bush.

'In 2000 in Florida, Bush won by 537 votes, and you got 97,488', Meet the Press host Tim Russert told Nader on air. 'In New Hampshire, Bush won by 7,211, you got 22,000 votes.'

In response, Nader said he did not cost Gore the election, because Gore won the election. Nader called his detractors the 'liberal intelligentsia' and said, 'what they're doing is basically saying that third parties are a second class citizenship'.

Nader said there is a 'civil liberties crisis' affecting third parties and Independent candidates, in the United States. 'Historically,' he said, 'that's where our reform has come from, in the 19th century, against slavery, women's right to vote, trade union, farmer, populist, progressive.'

Nader said both Republicans and Democrats are basically reading from the same playbook. 'They're taking our country apart: massive poverty, massive child poverty, massive consumer debt, environmental devastation. That didn't occur, that didn't get worse under the Democrats? So, basically, it's a question between both parties flunking, one with a D-, the Republicans; one with a D+, the Democrats.'

Environmental News Service, Washington D.C., 23 February 2004

Demographics of military mirror society as a whole

As a veteran, I found Brian Fejer's letter in the Aug. 23 Daily Lobo interesting to say the least, though it's obvious that he has never served in any of the U.S. armed forces. If he had, he would understand that the populations of these organizations have the same demographics as the population of the U.S. as a whole.

While I myself am frustrated by U.S. foreign policy, we should focus our frustrations on the ones that dictate policy, not the ones that are forced to carry out these policies, facing possible imprisonment for dereliction of the duty they volunteered for.

The men and women serving in the Middle East are your next door neighbors, teachers, and people that you meet in everyday life. While it's possible that some of those people could be bigots or drug addicts, the majority are professionals that are there to do a job, get paid and eventually go home to their families with a minimum of injuries and hopefully the ability to sleep at night.

Alex Fields, *New Mexico Daily Lobo*, 24 August 2006

Alcohol main cause of teen pregnancies

Unwanted teenage pregnancies following bouts of binge drinking are contributing to the world's unsustainable population growth, a World Health Organization academic says.

John Gillebaud, a leading academic on birth control, reproductive health, and population issues, told a conference in Canberra today that unprotected sex leading to unwanted pregnancies is the greatest threat to mankind.

'Every single week a new city of 1.7 million could be created, and the current global population growth is unsustainable,' he said via video link from London.

'Each year, there are around 80 million unwanted pregnancies and 30 million of these are aborted,' he said.

'The inconvenient truth is, the world is already overpopulated and soon we may experience shortages of food and water.'

Mr Gillebaud said reckless alcohol consumption was the main reason for unwanted teenage pregnancies.

'Alcohol causes more unwanted teenage pregnancies than anything else,' he said.

Liberal MP Mal Washer and outgoing chair of the parliamentary committee on population and development agreed with Mr Gillebaud, saying binge drinking was the leading cause of unwanted pregnancies among teenagers in Australia.

Mr Washer applauded the Rudd Government's $53 million binge drinking strategy.

The strategy includes a $20 million television, radio, and internet campaign to shock young people with the consequences of binge drinking.

'I fully back the Rudd Government on this issue, and I am sure it will go a long way in addressing the violence and irresponsible behaviour that binge drinking causes,' he said.

AAP, *The Australian*, 14 March 2008

5

Developing a position

Truth springs from argument amongst friends.

David Hume

We have now completed our survey of the formal and informal techniques for evaluating arguments. Applying these techniques, you will be able to bring down even the most sophisticated opponents, thereby laying the foundation for a constructive contribution of your own. In this last chapter we will investigate the three main steps for developing a position on an issue.

To illustrate these steps, we will use the vehicle of writing a position paper. A position paper is an essay putting forward opinions on an issue. Although this vehicle is most directly relevant to students, it is a skill of surprising importance in the workplace as well. Jobs in many different fields require you to present your view on controversial topics at meetings. While you probably wouldn't want to read a paper to your audience in this situation, you would do well to write out your thoughts in advance. It's easy to feel you have a foolproof proposal in mind until you open your mouth and find it coming out in a jumble! Thinking at the keyboard is a good way to learn how to organize your ideas. Once you have mastered the basic pattern for a good position paper, you will find yourself reasoning in the same cogent way even when there is no time to hit the keyboard.

The issues you face at work or in the classroom are likely to require insider knowledge impossible to simulate in this book.

So we'll look at a topic of universal interest that most everyone has some experience with, namely, romantic love.

Steven Pinker is a cognitive scientist at Harvard University. While one of the lead researchers in his field, he also has a rare talent for explaining science to non-scientists. In 1997, Pinker published a book called *How the Mind Works*, which sold millions of copies, won numerous awards, and was converted into a popular video-lecture series. In the book, Pinker presented provocative new theories of human behavior that have had lasting impact. In January 2008, *Time* magazine solicited Pinker's opinion about romantic love and he reconfirmed what he originally wrote about it more than ten years earlier in *How the Mind Works*. Let's have a look at Pinker's theory of romantic love and then develop a position of our own on the issue.

Explanation/reconstruction

The first step in writing a good position paper is reading. The more familiar you are with the issue, the more credible your arguments will be. This means reading around on the topic to learn about the range of views already out there.

As you think about the issue and begin to lean in one direction, identify the author who will serve as your primary opponent. Needless to say, you will encounter many approaches you disagree with. But you can't challenge them all, and you should be careful who you do challenge. In particular, be sure to resist the temptation to choose an opponent who would be easy to refute. This would be to commit a form of the straw man fallacy. Instead, you want to choose as your opponent the person you think represents the biggest threat to your own view. This will be someone who already enjoys a great deal of support from your colleagues or classmates and it will be someone with an excellent argument. Your opponent's argument should be so good that it may even cause you to reconsider or change your mind on the issue.

When you have identified your opponent, read what he or she says on the topic several times until you identify a crucial passage or set of passages that captures the heart of his or her argument. For the purpose of demonstration, we have selected two passages from Pinker's book, *How the Mind Works*.

In the first passage, Pinker provides a framework for his theory of romantic love. He writes:

> In this chapter I present a distinctly unromantic theory of the emotions. It combines the computational theory of the mind, which says that the lifeblood of the psyche is information rather than energy, with the modern theory of evolution, which calls for reverse-engineering the complex design of biological systems. I will show that the emotions are adaptations, well-engineered software modules that work in harmony with the intellect and are indispensable to the functioning of the whole mind. The problem with the emotions is not that they are untamed forces or vestiges of our animal past; it is that they were designed to propagate copies of the genes that built them rather than to promote happiness, wisdom, or moral values. We often call an act 'emotional' when it is harmful to the social group, damaging to the actor's happiness in the long run, uncontrollable and impervious to persuasion, or a product of self-delusion. Sad to say, these outcomes are not malfunctions but precisely what we would expect from well-engineered emotions.

S. Pinker, *How the Mind Works*
(New York: W.W. Norton, 1997), p. 370

Pinker intends to argue that human emotions, such as romantic love, are not malfunctions but rather clever devices engineered by evolution to propagate our species.

This passage is important because it shows how Pinker's theory of romantic love fits into his picture of human nature in general. Pinker tells us his theory is a combination of two scientific models. The first is computational theory, which says the mind is an information-processing machine like a computer. This enables Pinker to cast the emotions as indispensable 'software modules'. The second is evolution, which says today's human beings are the product of millions of years of survival of the fittest. All of the qualities we have, including emotional qualities, are adaptations to our environment that enabled us to reproduce successfully, thereby passing on our genes. Your position paper should begin with a general explanation of the author's approach that is sensitive to your audience. Depending on their level of expertise, you may need to define a number of key concepts, such as *software module*, *adaptation*, and *gene*.

Having laid out the territory, you are ready to proceed to the argument about romantic love. Later in the same chapter, Pinker writes,

> Why does romantic love leave us bewitched, bothered, and bewildered? Could it be another paradoxical tactic like handcuffing oneself to railroad tracks? Quite possibly. Offering to spend your life and raise children with someone is the most important promise you'll ever make, and a promise is most credible when the promiser can't back out. Here is how the economist Robert Frank has reverse-engineered mad love.
>
> Unsentimental social scientists and veterans of the singles scene agree that dating is a marketplace. People differ in their value as potential marriage partners. Almost everyone agrees that Mr or Ms Right should be good-looking, smart, kind, stable, funny, and rich. People shop for the most desirable person who will accept them, and that is why most marriages pair a bride and a groom of approximately equal desirability. Mate-shopping, however, is only part of the psychology of

romance; it explains the statistics of mate choice, but not the final pick. Somewhere in this world of five billion people there lives the best-looking, richest, smartest, funniest, kindest person who would settle for you. But your dreamboat is a needle in a haystack, and you may die single if you insist on waiting for him or her to show up. Staying single has costs, such as loneliness, childlessness, and playing the dating game with all its awkward drinks and dinners (and sometimes breakfasts). At some point it pays to set up house with the best person you have found so far.

But that calculation leaves your partner vulnerable. The laws of probability say that someday you will meet a more desirable person, and if you are always going for the best you can get, on that day you will dump your partner. But your partner has invested money, time, childrearing and forgone opportunities in the relationship. If your partner was the most desirable person in the world, he or she would have nothing to worry about, because you would never want to desert. But failing that, the partner would have been foolish to enter the relationship.

Frank compares the marriage market with the rental market. Landlords desire the best of all tenants but settle for the best they can find, and renters want the best of all apartments but settle for the best they can find. Each invests in the apartment (the landlord may paint it the tenant's favorite color; the tenant may install permanent decorations), so each would be harmed if the other suddenly terminated the agreement. If the tenant could leave for a better flat, the landlord would have to bear the costs of an unrented unit and the search for a new tenant; he would have to charge a high rent to cover that risk, and would be loath to paint. If the landlord could evict the tenant for a better one, the tenant would have to search for a new home; she would be willing to pay only a low rent, and would not bother to keep the apartment in good shape, if she had to expose herself to that risk. If the best tenant were renting the best apartment, the worries would be moot; neither would want to end the arrangement. But since both have to compromise, they protect themselves by signing a lease that is expensive for either to break. By agreeing to restrict his own freedom to evict, the landlord can charge a higher rent. By agreeing to restrict her own freedom to leave, the tenant can demand a lower rent. Lack of choice works to each one's advantage.

Marriage laws work a bit like leases, but our ancestors had to find some way to commit themselves before the laws existed. How can you be sure that a prospective partner won't leave the minute it is rational to do so – say, when a 10-out-of-10 moves in next door? One answer is, don't accept a partner who wanted you for rational reasons to begin with; look for a partner who is committed to staying with you because you are you. Committed by what? Committed by an emotion. An emotion that the person did not decide to have, and so cannot decide not to have. An emotion that was not triggered by your objective mate-value and so will not be alienated by someone with greater mate-value. An emotion that is guaranteed not to be a sham because it has physiological costs like tachycardia, insomnia, and anorexia. An emotion like romantic love.

'People who are sensible about love are incapable of it,' wrote Douglas Yates. Even when courted by the perfect suitor, people are unable to will themselves to fall in love, often to the bewilderment of the matchmaker, the suitor, and the person himself or herself. Instead it is a glance a laugh, a manner that steals the heart.

Ibid., pp. 417–18

In this passage, Pinker presents an explanation of romantic love that is consistent with his overall account of human nature.

Since romantic love is such a crazy, irrational experience, it seems to pose a threat to Pinker's computation-evolution model of the mind. If this model cannot explain romantic love, then it is deeply flawed. Pinker wants to show, however, that romantic love is exactly what we would expect the computation-evolution model to produce.

We can reconstruct Pinker's argument in standard form as follows:

1. The rental market is like the marriage market.
2. If the rental market is like the marriage market, then tenants and landlords are to leases just as spouses are to marriage vows.

---

3. So, tenants and landlords are to leases just as spouses are to marriage vows.
4. Leases protect long term investments.
5. Long term investments work to the advantage of tenants and landlords.

---

6. So, leases work to the advantage of tenants and landlords.

---

7. So, marriage vows work to the advantage of spouses.
8. If marriage vows work to the advantage of spouses, then evolution should design romantic love to be as restrictive as marriage vows.
9. If evolution should design romantic love to be as restrictive as marriage vows, then romantic love should make lovers immune to calculations about finding a better lover.
10. If romantic love should make lovers immune to calculations about finding a better lover, then it should be irrational.
11. If romantic love should be irrational, then it should be grounded in uncontrollable emotions.

---

12. So, romantic love should be grounded in uncontrollable emotions.

13. Romantic love actually is grounded in uncontrollable emotions.

14. Therefore, romantic love actually is exactly as it should be.

This standard form combines several different rules of inference. Steps 1 through 3 are modus ponens. Steps 4 through 6 are categorical syllogism. Step 3 and step 6 imply step 7 by analogy. Step 12 follows from step 7 along with steps 8 through 11 by modus ponens and hypothetical syllogism. The final conclusion, step 14, follows from steps 12 and 13 by categorical syllogism.

Notice that the second half of the argument employs a predictive sense of the word 'should'. By saying that evolution 'should' design romantic love to be as restrictive as marriage vows, Pinker means that, based on his computational account of evolution, *he would expect* romantic love to function that way. This is a common form of argument in the sciences: 'If my hypothesis is correct, then the results should turn out thus.' You will find the same kind of reasoning outside of science as well, wherever predictions are relevant.

Although we could have reconstructed Pinker's argument much more concisely, elaborating fourteen steps gives us a nice variety of points to work with in our evaluation. As with the editorial we wrote in chapter 3, we probably wouldn't actually insert the standard form in our position paper. We certainly wouldn't read it out loud at a meeting! Nevertheless, having spelled out the steps in Pinker's reasoning, we will now be able to conduct a much more effective analysis.

Objection/response

Once you have a good standard form to work with, pause to brainstorm a list of its strongest opponents.

First, who does Pinker see as his main opponent? In the first passage quoted above he wrote, 'The problem with the emotions is not that they are untamed forces or vestiges of our animal past; it is that they were designed to propagate copies of the genes that built them rather than to promote happiness, wisdom, or moral values'.

This suggests Pinker thinks of his main opponent as someone who agrees that today's humans are the product of survival of the fittest, but also thinks we still carry various unsuccessful traits. Because this opponent is unable to explain why romantic love would be a successful survival strategy, he or she can only dismiss it as an 'untamed force' or 'vestige of the past'. By showing how romantic love promotes reproduction, Pinker attempts to present a stronger case for evolution than does his opponent. He is asserting that even an unlikely trait like romantic love confirms the explanatory power of the principle of survival of the fittest.

Second, although Pinker doesn't mention it, his argument might serve to challenge an opponent who rejects evolution all together on the grounds that human beings still have so many apparently unfit traits. Someone who believed that evolution was supposed to produce happiness, wisdom, and moral values, would look around and see that it has not, and thereby reject the theory of evolution. Pinker's analysis of romantic love shows how evolution is geared toward maximizing reproduction, regardless of happiness, wisdom, and moral values. If he is right, then romantic love and other emotional aspects of human behavior can no longer serve as leverage against evolution.

Third, since Pinker's conclusion validates romantic love as a natural and even necessary part of human nature, someone who was critical of emotional behavior would oppose him. Stoics, for example, are those who believe human beings should try to minimize or eliminate all of their emotions. Convinced that rationality alone is the way to the good life, they would never approve of the idea that romantic love could have a benefit for our species. Likewise, one can imagine adherents of certain religions being opposed to Pinker's validation of romantic love.

As critical thinkers, we need to set aside any pre-existing biases we may be harboring either for or against our author's proposal and evaluate it based on the strength of the reasons he advances on its behalf. Having brainstormed some general sources of opposition we should now launch a specific critique of Pinker's reasons.

Pinker's reasons have become the premises of our standard form reconstruction. Remember that, while any premise is open to objection, it is pointless to target a premise that is also a subconclusion. Subconclusions follow from preceding steps. So, if there is a problem with the subconclusion, you have to locate the source of that problem somewhere in the preceding steps.

Furthermore, if you find yourself inclined to target something the author said in the passage that is not reflected in your standard form, then your standard form is inadequate. The whole point of the standard form is to isolate all of the controversial claims the conclusion hinges on so that you can select one as your primary target. If you left something crucial out of the standard form, then you need to rewrite it or expand it accordingly.

The first premise of the standard form may constitute a suitable target. It states: the rental market is like the marriage market. Pinker supports this premise with a series of comments at the beginning of the second quoted passage. He writes,

> Unsentimental social scientists and veterans of the singles scene agree that dating is a marketplace. People differ in their value as potential marriage partners. Almost everyone agrees that Mr or Ms Right should be good-looking, smart, kind, stable, funny, and rich. People shop for the most desirable person who will accept them, and that is why most marriages pair a bride and a groom of approximately equal desirability.

As critical thinkers, we might be alerted to a number of possible fallacies in this passage.

First, ad verecundiam, the fallacy of relying on an inappropriate authority, is a concern. Pinker cites unsentimental social scientists and veterans of the singles scene as authorities on dating. Since he doesn't footnote any studies, we know he is speaking loosely when he suggests they all agree dating is a marketplace. Suppose he's right that most do. Are they liable to be accurate sources of information? Veterans of the singles scene will consist of those who either tried and failed to marry or never wanted to marry in the first place. One could argue that they are liable to hold an uninformed or biased view about relationships. A similar problem arises with unsentimental social scientists. We need to know how to define 'unsentimental'. If 'unsentimental' ends up referring to those who have had serious problems with relationships, then they may not be a trustworthy source.

Second, we might worry about ad populum in this passage. Pinker states that 'Almost everyone agrees that Mr or Ms Right should be good-looking, smart, kind, stable, funny, and rich'. Is this true? And even if it is true, does it matter? There are so many differing opinions on what counts as good-looking, smart, kind, stable, funny, and rich that the agreement may be meaningless in practice. This is an important problem because Pinker uses the alleged universal agreement about Mr or Ms Right to establish the claim that there is an objective marriage-value scale upon which people can be ranked.

Third, the passage may beg the question. Pinker states that 'People shop for the most desirable person who will accept them, and that is why most marriages pair a bride and a groom of approximately equal desirability'. Do most marriages pair a bride and a groom of approximately equal desirability? In order to know this we would have to have an objective marriage scale on which to rank people. But this is the very claim Pinker is trying to prove. A marketplace is a venue in which people shop for goods that are given a price – which is an objective value scale. So, it seems Pinker may be arguing in a circle: dating is a marketplace because it is a venue in which people shop for goods on an objective value, and it is a venue in which people shop for goods on an objective value because it is a marketplace. An opponent who denied dating involves such ranking would not be able to get past the first step of Pinker's argument.

So far, we've learned that the analogy comparing renting to dating crucially depends on considerations that may commit one or more of the informal fallacies. Of course, the informal fallacies are subjective, meaning that they depend on context and purpose. Pinker could respond that he wished to introduce his argument with a lighthearted tone in order to capture the reader's attention, and that the real meat of the argument comes later. After all, Pinker himself tells us that the analogy ultimately comes from economist Robert Frank. It is designed to provide support for premise 7, that marriage vows work to the advantage of spouses. But this premise is not terribly controversial and could be supported on other grounds. We should therefore see whether the remainder of the standard form is sound.

Premise 9 might be vulnerable to attack. It states:

> If evolution should design romantic love to be as restrictive as
> marriage vows, then romantic love should make lovers immune
> to calculations about finding a better lover.

This is a conditional statement. Recall that, in order to refute a conditional statement, one has to show that the antecedent could be true while the consequent is false. As opponents of Pinker, we might agree that evolution should design romantic love to be as restrictive as marriage vows but disagree that it should do this by making lovers immune to calculations about finding a better lover. On closer consideration it seems evident that marriage vows don't actually make lovers immune to calculations about finding a better lover. Rather, they prevent lovers from *acting on* such calculations – and they don't even do that very effectively! It could be that being able to make calculations about finding a better lover is actually a good thing from an evolutionary perspective.

Consider the fact that many species of animals are not monogamous at all. Our near relatives the chimpanzees, for example, are notoriously promiscuous. They don't need to form stable family units because their offspring become independent relatively quickly. Human children, in contrast, need many years of nurturing to have any hope of survival on their own. This may well be why our species tends towards monogamy. But the operative word here is 'tends'. The truth is that raising children does not require monogamy.

On the contrary, there is evidence that natural selection has favored multiple mates for our species. As the award-winning science writer Carl Zimmer points out, recent studies of human DNA make

> a powerful case that polygyny has been common for tens of thousands of years across the Old World. It's possible that polygyny was an open institution for much of that time, or that secret trysts made it a reality that few would acknowledge. What's much less possible is that monogamy has been the status quo for 50,000 years.
>
> C. Zimmer, 'Adam and his Eves', *The Loom*,
> (http://blogs.discovermagazine.com/loom/2004/08/23/
> adam-and-his-eves/), 2004

If human beings have been chasing illicit liaisons since the beginning, and this has enabled us to overpopulate the globe, then it seems evolution has not favored monogamy.

So, the fundamental problem that emerges from careful thought about premise 7 is that romantic love does not need to be nearly as restrictive as Pinker suggests. Toward the end of the passage from *How the Mind Works*, Pinker writes,

> How can you be sure that a prospective partner won't leave the minute it is rational to do so – say, when a 10-out-of-10 moves in next door? One answer is, don't accept a partner who wanted you for rational reasons to begin with; look for a partner who is committed to staying with you because you are you. Committed by what? Committed by an emotion. An emotion that the person did not decide to have, and so cannot decide not to have. An emotion that was not triggered by your objective mate-value and so will not be alienated by someone with greater mate-value.

It seems Pinker is neglecting the fact that evolution seems to actually favor cheating, suggesting that, for survival fitness, the mated members of our species need not be, and often are not, immune to calculations about finding a better lover.

This line of reasoning could lead to a powerful objection against Pinker's argument. It would require a good deal more research and elaboration to be completely convincing. We have said enough, however, for the purpose of illustration.

The important point to appreciate at this juncture is that even the most powerful objection against an argument is dubious if the author is not allowed to respond. After working out the best attack on the author you can muster, always pause to consider how the author would respond before proceeding to the final stage of your paper. Sometimes when you do this, you'll find the author has such a good response that your objection begins to look like an instance of straw man. In that case, it will be wise to go back to the drawing board and develop a different objection. Other times, in searching for the author's response, you may discover something new that takes the debate to a deeper level.

Notice how our objection raises a concrete counter-example to premise 9. Our objection aims to show that the widespread phenomenon of adultery proves romantic love should not make human beings immune to calculations about finding a better lover. It might be tempting for Pinker to ignore this counter-example, generating a different example in support of his thesis instead. For instance, he might argue that religion could provide another way to make human beings immune to calculations about finding another lover. Religion is a common denominator among human beings in every corner of the globe, and has been since the dawn of civilization. Although religions are different, most glorify faithfulness in marriage and punish sexual transgressions.

While religion could become relevant to this discussion at some stage, it would be a mistake for Pinker to use it as a response to the adultery objection. Fighting one example with a different example is a version of the red herring fallacy because the effect is to change the subject. Changing the subject in this way is a very common error in a position paper and critical thinkers must avoid it at all costs. There is already an objection on the table. Pinker must respond *to that very objection* or we will be inclined to suspect it has him beat.

So, what would Pinker say about the adultery example? It seems his best bet would be to clarify what he meant by 'commitment'. A man might feel deeply committed to his family unit even while sowing wild oats with the 10-out-of-10 who moved in next door. By defining 'commitment' loosely, Pinker can consistently concede that human beings are prone to cheating. After all, what 'cheating' means is that the person wants to retain the original relationship while at the same time getting extra on the side. Pinker's point is that the desire to retain the original relationship is enforced by the deeply irrational emotional attachment of romantic love. Pinker would pose the question: why do human beings bother to cheat, when they could simply walk out? His theory provides an answer: heart-strings pull them back, even if going back defies all rational calculation. Of course, humans sometimes do dump one partner in favor of a higher-ranking alternative. But notice that, in such cases, people often say 'she never really loved him', or 'he was just using her all along'. This suggests that true cases of romantic love prevent or at least strongly deter dumping – even while they permit cheating.

In order to complete our defense of Pinker, it would be best to find some concrete empirical evidence for our claims. We may also want to read other things Pinker has written for clues to how he might defend himself. For present purposes, however, we shall pass on to the final stage of the paper.

Resolution

Once you have exhausted your resources for objection and response, you are in a position to make an intelligent determination of your own on the question. Only after you have examined both sides with an open mind will you be able to make a worthwhile contribution to the debate. Which side do you ultimately find the most compelling and why? Or have you found that both sides have problems that a third possibility might solve?

Don't think of the resolution section of your paper as your concluding paragraph. You should add a brief summary conclusion *after* the resolution section of your paper. The resolution is not a throwaway afterthought in which to reveal a bias. On the contrary, it is the most important section of the paper – its raison d'être! The explanation, the reconstruction, the objection, and the response to the objection all lead up to the moment when you finally make your case for your own view. This means not just stating an opinion but making an argument: you need to present a clear proposal with reasons to support it.

To put yourself in the right frame of mind, you may want to try plugging your ideas into a standard form. As you no doubt realize by now, the standard form is just a device for setting your logic straight. When it comes time for you to make your case at a meeting or in class you shouldn't need it. It will have done its job by then and will help you express yourself effectively.

What is your view of romantic love? We leave it to you to finish this paper on your own.

Exercises

Try your hand at writing a position paper on the following selections. Start with an explanation of the issue. This will involve reading the selection several times and defining key terms. Next, reconstruct the author's argument in valid standard form. Then, select the premise you find most controversial for an objection and a response. When you feel you have fully examined both sides of the issue, make a case for your own view. Finally, add a brief introduction and a brief conclusion.

Law

As an international human rights lawyer and academic who has only recently returned from Washington, I find . . . that for many political actors, including in the Washington political environment, rules of international law are more nuisance than guide. There definitely is a strong and discernible impulse to subordinate law to power and lawyers to their political clients. But if there is one lesson that I have learned, it is that the transnational legal process of norm-internalisation is not self-activating. If international relations are to be more than just power politics, international lawyers must serve as moral actors, who seek self-consciously to promote this process of norm-internalisation. It is the job of international lawyers to promote international norms, to identify legal constraints and to identify ways to channel proposed state actions into normative frameworks. By so doing, public international lawyers help shape policy decisions, which in turn shape legal instruments, which in time become internalised into bureaucratic decision-making processes that promote national compliance with international norms. By so doing, international lawyers who work in the public interest can influence policy, and help influence the development of transnational public law.

> H.H. Koh, 'Opening Remarks: Transnational Legal Processes Illuminated', in Michael Likosky (ed.), *Transnational Legal Processes: Globalisation and Power Disparities* (London: Butterworths LexisNexis, 2002), p. 332

Anthropology

The pig had been domesticated for one purpose only, namely to supply meat. As ecological conditions became unfavourable for pig raising, there was no alternative function which could redeem its existence. The creature became not only useless, but worse than useless – harmful, a curse to touch or merely to see – a pariah animal . . .

In this perspective, the fact that pig raising remained possible for the Israelites at low cost in certain remnant hillside forests of swampy habitats, or at extra expense where shade and water were scarce, does not contradict the ecological basis of the taboo. If there had not been some minimum possibility of raising pigs, there would have been no reason to taboo the practice. As the history of Hindu cow protection shows, religions gain strength when they help people make decisions which are in accord with pre-existing useful practices, but which are not so completely self-evident as to preclude doubts and temptations. To judge from the Eight-fold Way or the Ten Commandments, God does not usually waste time prohibiting the impossible or condemning the unthinkable . . .

If the Israelites had been alone in their interdictions of pork, I would find it more difficult to choose among alternative explanations of the pig taboo. The recurrence of pig aversions in several different Middle Eastern cultures strongly supports the view that the Israelite ban was a response to recurrent practical conditions rather than to a set of beliefs peculiar to one religion's notions about clean and unclean animals. At least three other important Middle Eastern civilizations – the Phoenicians, Egyptians, and Babylonians – were as disturbed by pigs as were the Israelites.

Marvin Harris, 'The Abominable Pig', in Carole Counihan and Penny Van Esterik, (eds), *Food and Culture: A Reader*, 2nd edn (Routledge, 2008), pp. 60–4

Philosophy

The existentialist's turn away from abstract principles is often taken to imply that there are no such principles proper to existentialist thought. If this were the case, then the only accurate way to explain existentialist thought would be to recount the descriptions of concrete life found in the works of existentialist authors, along with the technical terminology used in these descriptions. And, in fact, existentialist authors dedicate a great deal of their writings to the explication of such concrete details. Hence, the apparent propriety of focusing a supplemental study on these details, and this is the approach that such studies typically take. The result, however, is usually a welter of statements about the complexity of everyday life, about the difficulties intrinsic to concrete human existence, along with loosely connected discussions of the vast array of technical terms employed by existentialist authors to describe these phenomena. In this way the reader is given the impression that the disunity suffered by supplemental studies that take this approach is inherent in existentialist thought itself. Existentialism seems to be composed of a loosely connected group of writers, without any principles to tie them together. Moreover, this characterization promotes a stereotypical view of existentialism that has cast suspicion on its properly philosophical character, on the extent to which existentialist philosophy is really a philosophy at all. The stereotypical view is that existentialist authors eschew the entire apparatus of traditional philosophical analysis, by refusing to ground their claims about the nature of the world and of the human being in underlying principles. Instead existentialists are seen as promulgating their own peculiar, idiosyncratic views of the world, which are based on their parochial observations of the human condition – views that are then presented to their readers through a fog of obscure technical terminology.

By grounding existentialist thought in the basic principle of the indeterminacy of all that exists, and by deriving from this principle the specific doctrines regarding the nature of the world and of the human being held by existentialist philosophers, we hope to give a unified picture of the existentialist movement, and to take a step toward overcoming the stereotypical view of existentialism.

> Mark Tanzer, *On Existentialism* (Belmont CA: Thomson Wadsworth, 2008), p. 10

Conclusion

He who knows only his own side of the case knows little of that.

John Stuart Mill

Your mind is your most valuable asset. Critical thinking is the only way to take advantage of its ability to lead you to the truth.

In a free society where everyone has the right to believe and say almost anything they please, it is easy to lose sight of the importance of the truth. After all, the truth is often rather unpleasant. Why should we work so hard at trying to find it?

If you're not actively working at discovering the truth every time you think about an issue, then there's a very good chance you believe falsehoods. This should alarm you. It's counterproductive and even dangerous to tote falsehoods around in your mind because they can cause you to take the wrong action.

A simple example: suppose someone believes illness is caused by demons rather than germs. After he uses a public restroom, he whispers an incantation against the demons instead of washing his hands to remove the germs. Not surprisingly, this person has a tendency to catch colds a lot and to spread them to his family and friends. If he thought critically about his demon belief and discovered the truth he could avoid this unfortunate state of affairs.

Very few people believe in demons any more. But don't kid yourself into thinking you're free of false beliefs! Notice that the saddest thing about our demon guy is that, even after getting sick, he'll never realize the true cause. He'll simply assume he forgot to say the right incantation at the right time.

People who don't take critical thinking seriously are just like the demon guy. They find themselves miserable and they don't know why. They keep making the same mistakes over and over again, never getting to the truth of the matter.

Critical thinking cannot promise you a happy life. It can't even promise to reveal the truth. But it can promise to be much more conducive to both of these things than the alternative.

John Stuart Mill was a great nineteenth-century English philosopher who not only wrote important and influential theories about how human beings can improve their lives, but also put these theories into practice as a Member of Parliament and political activist. In an inaugural address to the University of St Andrews he presented what may be the best rallying cry for logic ever written. It is worth quoting him in full:

> Of logic I venture to say, even if limited to that of mere ratio-cination, the theory of names, propositions, and the syllogism, that there is no part of intellectual education which is of greater value, or whose place can so ill be supplied by anything else. Its uses, it is true, are chiefly negative; its function is, not so much to teach us to go right, as to keep us from going wrong. But in the operations of the intellect it is so much easier to go wrong than right; it is so utterly impossible for even the most vigorous mind to keep itself in the path but by maintaining a vigilant watch against all deviations, and noting all the byways by which it is possible to go astray – that the chief difference between one reasoner and another consists in their less or greater liability to be misled. Logic points out all the possible ways in which, start-ing from true premises, we may draw false conclusions. By its analysis of the reasoning process, and the forms it supplies for stating and setting forth our reasonings, it enables us to guard

the points at which a fallacy is in danger of slipping in, or to lay our fingers upon the place where it has slipped in. When I consider how very simple the theory of reasoning is, and how short a time is sufficient for acquiring a thorough knowledge of its principles and rules, and even considerable adeptness in applying them, I can find no excuse for omission to study it on the part of any one who aspires to succeed in any intellectual pursuit. Logic is the great disperser of hazy and confused thinking; it clears up the fogs which hide from us our own ignorance, and make us believe that we understand a subject when we do not. We must not be led away by talk about inarticulate giants who do great deeds without knowing how, and see into the most recondite truths without any of the ordinary helps, and without being able to explain to other people how they reach their conclusions, nor consequently to convince any other people of the truth of them. There may be such men, as there are deaf and dumb persons who do clever things, but for all that, speech and hearing are faculties by no means to be dispensed with. If you want to know whether you are thinking rightly, put your thoughts into words. In the very attempt to do this you will find yourselves, consciously or unconsciously, using logical forms. Logic compels us to throw our meaning into distinct propositions and our reasonings into distinct steps. It makes us conscious of all the implied assumptions on which we are proceeding and which, if not true, vitiate the entire process. It makes us aware what extent of doctrine we commit ourselves to by any course of reasoning, and obliges us to look the implied premises in the face, and make up our minds whether we can stand to them. It makes our opinions consistent with themselves and with one another, and forces us to think clearly, even when it cannot make us think correctly. It is true that error may be consistent and systematic as well as truth; but this is not the common case. It is no small advantage to see clearly the principles and consequences involved in our opinions, and which we must either accept, or else abandon those opinions. We are much nearer to finding truth when we search for it in broad daylight.

> J.S. Mill, 'Inaugural Address to St Andrews', *The Collected Works of John Stuart Mill*, Vol. XXI, ed. J.M. Robson (London: Routledge and Kegan Paul, 1984), pp. 658–9

Logic banishes darkness and lets in the light. There is no doubt that the success of civilization has always and will always continue to depend on it.

Now that you have worked through this book, you are ready to see the difference logic can make. Have another look at the lawyer's summation speech from the introduction. When you reread it now, the errors should jump off the page at you.

Exercise answer key

Introduction

Ladies and Gentlemen of the Jury,

We have heard testimony over the past several days regarding the brutal murder of Cassandra Thomas, the owner of a corner grocery store in Gamerton. Ms Thomas was shot dead in her store on the afternoon of 10 July.

The defendant, Mr Vincent Cockley, insists he had no motive for this crime. Yet he is in debt and his ex-girlfriend attests to his psychological instability.[1] Furthermore, although he has worked at the same company for five years, his co-workers say they feel they don't really know him.[2]

Mr Cockley's lawyer asks us to believe that Mr Cockley is just a shy little fellow who couldn't hurt a fly.[3] But the bottom line is this: either Mr Cockley is an upstanding citizen or he is violent criminal.[4] And a man who hasn't even paid his taxes for the past two years cannot be considered an upstanding citizen, shy or otherwise.

Everyone knows lying is wrong.[5] Yet Mr Cockley admitted that he lied to the police when they first questioned him concerning his whereabouts on the night of 10 July. Upon further questioning, the police learned that Mr. Cockley was in the process of planning a trip to Mexico – which very nearly enabled him to escape arrest.[6]

Mr Cockley testified that the trip was for a charity that helps needy people build homes. The charity organizer, however, testified that the construction crew is composed primarily of ex-cons. This confirms the well known fact that criminals habitu-ally associate with other criminals.[7]

Mr Cockley claims that on the night of 10 July, he arrived at Ms Thomas's store just as the real killer was fleeing and that he chased the killer across town before losing him. I must remind you, however, that Mr Cockley has already lied once. How can we be expected to believe anything else he tells us?[8]

Finally, the crime scene investigators have established that Ms Thomas's murderer wore the gloves displayed in Exhibit A. If the gloves did not fit Mr Cockley, then he would be proven innocent. But the gloves do fit him, as you witnessed with your own eyes. Therefore, Mr Cockley is guilty.[9] And therefore, he should receive the maximum penalty.[10]

Introduction – errors

1 Ad verecundiam: an ex-girlfriend is not an authority on Mr Cockley's psychological state. On the contrary, she is likely to be biased.

2 Ad ignorantiam: lack of proof about Mr Cockley's character does not prove he has bad character.

3 Straw man: this reduces the other lawyer's description of Mr. Cockley to an absurd caricature.

4 False dilemma: there are plenty of other possibilities between 'upstanding citizen' and 'violent criminal'.

5 Ad populum: regardless of what everyone allegedly thinks, there may be justified instances of lying.

6 Post hoc: because the trip was to occur *after* the murder, the lawyer assumes it was to occur *because of* the murder – as a means of escape. But the timing of the trip may just be a coincidence.

7 Begging the question: the principle is confirmed only if Mr Cockley is in fact a criminal, which is the very thing the lawyer is trying to prove.

8　Hasty generalization: one instance of lying does not make a person an inveterate liar.

9　Fallacy of denying the antecedent:

  1. If not-F, then not-G.

  2. F.

  ————————————————

  3. Therefore, G.

10　Is-ought fallacy: even if Mr Cockley is guilty, we have no reason for concluding that he ought to receive the maximum penalty.

Chapter 1

Cultural studies

1. Smog-breathing is to a smoggy place just as individual prejudice is to racist society.

2. Smog-breathing is an inescapable consequence of living in a smoggy place.

————————————————————————

3. Therefore, individual prejudice is an inescapable consequence of living in a racist society.

1. Running in the other direction is to the moving walkway just as active antiracism is to racism.

2. Unless you run in the other direction, you will be carried along with the moving walkway.

————————————————————————

3. Therefore, unless you are actively antiracist, you will be carried along with racism.

Aesthetics

1. Friendship is to a person just as appreciation is to artwork.

2. One cannot befriend a person with ethical defects.

---

3. Therefore, one cannot appreciate artwork with ethical defects.

Literature

1. Swift is to eighteenth-century England just as Hawthorne is to Lincoln.
2. Swift wrote ironic editorial notes to criticize eighteenth-century England.

---

3. Therefore, Hawthorne wrote ironic editorial notes to criticize Lincoln.

Chapter 2

The fifteen valid syllogisms

Barbara

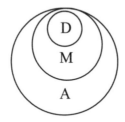

Celarent

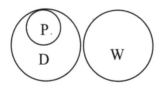

Darii

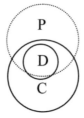

The circle for (P) is a dotted line on this diagram because premise 2 does not tell us exactly how to draw it. In particular, we don't know whether there are pets other than dogs that are colorblind, as this drawing indicates. Nevertheless, premise 2 gives us enough information to know that, *however we draw the circle for 'pets',* it *will have to* intersect with the circle for 'color-blind', which is the conclusion of the syllogism.

Ferio

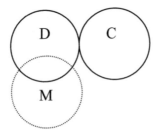

The circle for 'members of the police force' is a dotted line on this diagram because premise 2 does not tell us exactly how to draw it. For example, it doesn't tell us whether some members of the police department are able to drive a car, in which case we would move the circle labeled 'M' over so that it intersected with the circle labeled 'C'. Although premise 2 does not give us *complete* information, it gives us *enough* information to know that, however we draw the circle labeled 'M', the conclusion of the syllogism, that some members of the police force are not able to drive a car, will come out true.

Cesare

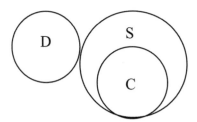

Camestres

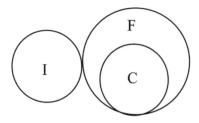

Festino

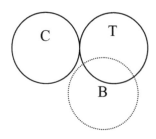

The circle for 'critters in these boxes', (B), is a dotted line on this diagram because premise 2 does not tell us exactly how to draw it. By telling us that some of the critters in the box can talk, it seems to imply that some *can't*. But 'some can' does not necessarily imply 'some can't', just as we saw in our example about the unfriendly armadillo. For example, suppose it turns out that there is just one critter in the box. Then the circle for (B) should be entirely enclosed within the circle for (T). At any rate, it doesn't matter for our purposes. No matter how we draw the circle for premise 2, we will *have to* draw it so that some of the members of (B) are not members of (C), which is the conclusion of the syllogism.

Baroco

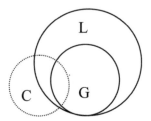

The circle for 'cats' is dotted on this diagram because premise 2 does not tell us exactly how to draw it. By saying that some cats are not loveable, it seems to imply that some cats *are* loveable, but – again – not necessarily! Although the circle for premise 2 can be drawn in a number of different ways, no matter how we draw it, part of (C) must lie outside (G), which is exactly what the conclusion says.

Disamis

The circle for 'beautiful' is dotted on this diagram because premise 1 does not tell us whether some iguanas are not beautiful. Nor does it tell us whether some of the lizards that are not

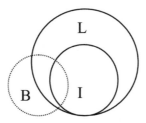

iguanas are beautiful, nor whether there are beautiful things that are not lizards at all. Regardless of how these questions are answered, we know that at least one member of (L) is also a member of (B), which is the conclusion of the syllogism.

Datisi

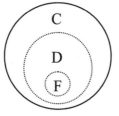

The circle for (D) is dotted on this diagram because premise 1 does not tell us whether there are collies *not* on this farm. The circle for (F) is dotted because premise 2 does not tell us whether some of the dogs on this farm are *not* feral. Regardless of how either of these issues is resolved, we know that there is at least one member of (C) that is also a member of (F), which is the conclusion of the syllogism.

Bocardo

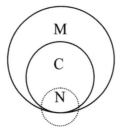

The circle for 'non-meat eaters', (N), is dotted on this diagram because we do not know everything this set includes. Regardless, we know it includes some mammals.

Ferison

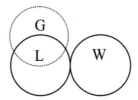

The circle for 'guaranteed to work on any animal' is dotted on this diagram because we don't know whether some leashes are *not* guaranteed to work on any animal, but this does not prevent us from seeing that the conclusion of the syllogism has to be true.

Camenes

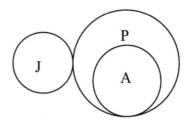

Dimaris

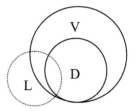

Do some lizards dwell outside the desert? And, if so, are they still victims of global warming or not? The premises do not tell us. Based on what they do tell us, however, we know for sure that some victims of global warming are lizards.

Fresison

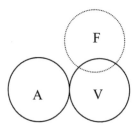

Are there farmers who are not going to vote for this policy? And, if so, are they animal lovers or not? We don't know. But we do know that the farmers who are voting for this policy are not animal lovers.

Chapter 2

Classics

1. Concern for the gods was central to farming and fighting.
2. Farming and fighting was central to the lives of the Athenian people.

3. Therefore, concern for the gods was central to the lives of the Athenian people.

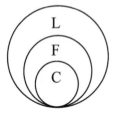

Philosophy

This passage invites us to construct a 'double-decker' Barbara syllogism by using the conclusion of the first syllogism as the first premise of the second syllogism.

1. The philosophers are those who are in the best state of mind.
2. Those who are in the best state of mind are dearest to the gods.

---

3. So, the philosophers are the dearest to the gods.
4. Those who are dearest to the gods are the happiest people.

---

5. Therefore, the philosophers are the happiest people.

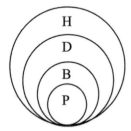

Religion

This passage, like the last, invites a double-decker Barbara syllogism. Someone may challenge its validity, however, on the grounds that 'is associated with' is not transitive.

1. Sex is associated with the body.
2. The body is associated with impermanence.

---

3. So, sex is associated with impermanence.
4. Impermanence is scorned by religion.

---

5. Therefore, sex is scorned by religion.

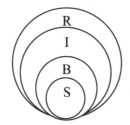

Chapter 3

Trade pact saps manufacturing jobs

1. If NAFTA were really a free trade agreement, then it would contain a page or two on eliminating tariffs.
2. NAFTA does not contain any pages on eliminating tariffs.

---

3. Therefore, NAFTA is not really a free trade agreement.
   [Modus tollens]

Act now to save the salmon

1. If we hope to save the salmon, then we must do two things: stop the rise in greenhouse gasses and secure our waters' health.
2. We do hope to save the salmon.

---

3. Therefore, we must do two things: stop the rise in greenhouse gasses and secure our waters' health.
   [Modus ponens]

Bonus baby

1. Either Blackwell's failure to provide his successor the most complete rundown of the administrative state of the office was an innocent oversight, or it was done consciously.
2. If it was an innocent oversight, then it bespeaks lack of seriousness.
3. If it was done consciously, then it bespeaks pettiness unworthy of a public servant in state office.

---

4. Therefore, Blackwell's failure to provide his successor the most complete rundown of the administrative state of the office bespeaks either lack of seriousness or pettiness unworthy of a public servant.
   [Constructive dilemma]

Closing the achievement gap

To prove: We must do something.
1. Suppose we do nothing.
2. If we do nothing, then statewide budget cuts will deepen existing inequities.
3. But it is unacceptable to allow budget cuts to deepen existing inequalities.

---

4. Therefore, we must do something.
   [An adaptation of reductio ad absurdum that uses the prescriptive notion of 'unacceptable' instead of the descriptive notion of 'absurd']

The *Nature* editorial

1. The editors are asserting either that there is evidence against intelligent design or that intelligent design is mistaken from a non-scientific standpoint.

2. If they are asserting that there is evidence against intelligent design, then they are admitting intelligent design is a real science.
3. If they are asserting that intelligent design is mistaken from a non-scientific standpoint, then they are advancing an atheistic theology.

---

4. Therefore, the editors are either admitting intelligent design is a real science or advancing an atheistic theology.
[Constructive dilemma]

No retreat from the War on Terror

1. If Britain talks of withdrawal, then Canada will withdraw.
2. If Canada withdraws, then Britain will withdraw.
3. If Britain withdraws, then the US will withdraw.
4. If the US withdraws, then the Afghan government will collapse.
5. If the Afghan government collapses, then Pakistan will become unstable.
6. If Pakistan becomes unstable, then everyone will feel the impact.

---

7. Therefore, if Britain talks of withdrawal, then everyone will feel the impact.
[Hypothetical syllogism—with multiple iteration]

Why Israel must kvetch

1. If defending Israel's image were a priority for Olmert, then he would regularly criticize the behavior of his 'peace partner' Abbas.
2. Olmert does not criticize the behavior of his 'peace partner' Abbas.

---

3. Therefore, defending Israel's image is not a priority for Olmert.
[Modus tollens]

Chapter 4

History lesson

The statement 'Perhaps Scott Rowed doesn't know that the U.S. Supreme Court twice – in 1964 and 1969 – defined humanism as a religion' could be an instance of equivocation on the word 'humanism'.

The statement 'That is the height of arrogance and ignorance combined' could be an instance of abusive ad hominem.

The phrase 'where everything Christian is rendered fit for attack' could be an instance of hasty generalization.

The statement 'Our whole educational system originated in the Catholic Church' could be an instance of ad verecundiam.

If not now, when?

The statement 'We all know that Ohio is in economic trouble' could be an instance of ad populum.

The statement 'Polls indicate that young professionals favor locating in cities that are welcoming to diversity' could be an instance of ad populum.

Heather Mills: a greedy woman hits the divorce jackpot

The phrase 'draw the nutters as surely as steaming cow patties do flies' could be an instance of poisoning the well.

The statement 'Although she strongly denied it, her case boils down to the syndrome of "Me too" or, "If he has it, I want it too"' could be an instance of straw man.

The phrase 'This is a greedy woman' could be an instance of abusive ad hominem.

The author may be accusing Heather Mills of committing the is–ought fallacy when she says that Mills 'at the ripe old age of 40, after a marriage that lasted all of four years, decided that she should not have to work ever again'.

The phrase 'went after the ex with that special viciousness forged in the bedroom' could be an instance of circumstantial ad hominem.

Global warming, or global con?

The title of this article could be an instance of false dilemma.

In the statement 'It is a 'consensus' in that it started with a foregone conclusion – that man-made pollution is dooming the planet – and gathered in any and all opinions that supported it' the author is accusing the Intergovernmental Panel of begging the question.

The statement 'It would achieve this trifling result only at the cost of literally trillions of dollars over that time – money that will not come from some imaginary place or "global resources", but out of your pocket' could be an instance of the fallacy of division.

The statement 'After all, when the U.N. grandly says "we must work together", what it's really saying is, "Americans must foot the bill"' could be an instance of straw man.

Nader jumps into the Presidential race

The statement 'Nader said he did not cost Gore the election, because Gore won the election' could contain an instance of equivocation on the word 'won'.

The phrase 'liberal intelligentsia' could be an instance of poisoning the well.

The statement 'what they're doing is basically saying that third parties are a second class citizenship' could be an instance of straw man.

The statement 'both Republicans and Democrats are basically reading from the same playbook' could be an instance of straw man.

Demographics of military mirror society as a whole

The statement 'it's obvious that he has never served in any of the U.S. armed forces. If he had, he would understand' could be an instance of ad ignorantiam.

The statement 'the populations of these organizations have the same demographics as the population of the U.S. as a whole' could be an instance of the fallacy of composition.

Alcohol main cause of teen pregnancies

The statement 'Mr Gillebaud said reckless alcohol consumption was the main reason for unwanted teenage pregnancies' could be an instance of post hoc. (Is there a common cause of both behaviors?)

The statement 'Alcohol causes more unwanted teenage pregnancies than anything else' could be an instance of amphiboly. Due to poor grammatical structure, it could mean two different things:

1. Alcohol, more than anything else, causes unwanted teenage pregnancies.
2. Alcohol causes unwanted teenage pregnancy more than it causes anything else.

The statement 'Liberal MP Mal Washer and outgoing chair of the parliamentary committee on population and development agreed with Mr Gillebaud, saying binge drinking was the leading cause of unwanted pregnancies among teenagers in Australia' could contain an instance of ad verecundiam. A member of parliament is not an expert in sociology.

The 'television, radio and internet campaign to shock young people with the consequences of binge drinking' could commit the fallacy ad baculum or the fallacy ad misericordiam depending on whether it uses threats or guilt to make its case.

Glossary

Antecedent   the 'If . . ' part of a conditional statement

Argument   a discussion in which reasons are advanced in favor of a proposal

Argument by analogy   an argument that draws a conclusion about one thing based on its likeness to another thing

Begging the question   to assume (as a premise) the very same thing you are trying to prove (in the conclusion).

Conclusion   the final step of an argument

Conditional statement   a statement of the form 'If . . . then . . .'

Consequent   the 'then . . .' part of a conditional statement

Critical thinking   the mental habit of checking your own logic as well as the logic of others

Counterfactual conditional statement   tells how the world would be if its antecedent were true

Deductive argument   a line of reasoning that produces a necessary conclusion

Descriptive statement   tells how the world is

Fallacy   a mistake in reasoning

Inductive argument   a line of reasoning that produces only a probable conclusion

Middle term connects the subject term to the predicate term in a syllogism without appearing in the conclusion

Normative statement see prescriptive statement

Particular affirmative a categorical statement of the form 'Some Xs are Y'

Particular negative a categorical statement of the form 'Some Xs are not-Y'

Position an opinion supported by argument

Predicate the phrase that affirms or denies something about the subject

Propositional logic see sentential logic

Predictive statement tells how the world will be

Premise the steps in an argument that imply the conclusion

Prescriptive statement tells how the world should be

Sentential logic studies the connections between different kinds of statements

Soundness when an argument (1) is valid and (2) has true premises

Standard form a schema for identifying the premises and conclusion of an argument

Subconclusion a conclusion that functions as a premise for a further conclusion

Subject the term in a statement about which something is affirmed or denied

Syllogism a three-step transitive argument

Theory of the categorical syllogism   studies the connections between categorical statements

Transitivity   a mathematical law according to which a relationship holds between the members of a sequence such that the middle members make a bridge from the first member to the last

Universal affirmative   a categorical statement of the form 'All Xs are Y'

Universal negative   a categorical statement of the form 'All Xs are not-Y (No X is Y)'

Validity   when the premises of an argument imply the conclusion such that, if the premises are true, the conclusion has to be true

Quick reference

Rules of inference

Argument by analogy

1. a : b :: c : d   ('a is to b just as c is to d')
2. a–P–b   ('a is related to b through P')

---

3. c–P–d   ('Therefore, c is related to d through P')

Transitivity

1. X is Y.
2. Y is Z.

---

3. Therefore, X is Z.

Hypothetical syllogism

1. If P, then Q.
2. If Q, then R.

---

3. Therefore, if P, then R.

Modus ponens

1. If P, then Q.
2. P.

---

3. Therefore, Q.

Modus tollens

1. If P, then Q.
2. Not-Q.

   _____

3. Therefore, not-P.

Reductio ad absurdum

To prove: Not-P
1. Suppose P.
2. If P, then Q.
3. But Q is absurd.

   _____

4. Therefore, not-P.

Disjunctive syllogism

1. Either P or Q.
2. Not-Q.

   _____

3. Therefore, P.

Constructive dilemma

1. Either P or Q.
2. If P, then R.
3. If Q, then S.

   _____

4. Therefore, either R or S.

Formal fallacies

In categorical syllogisms

1. Undistributed middle: neither of the premises accounts for all
   members of the category described by the middle term.

2. Illicit treatment of the predicate term: the premise containing the syllogism's predicate term fails to account for all the members of the category which that predicate term describes.
3. Illicit treatment of the subject term: the premise containing the syllogism's subject term fails to account for all the members of the category which that subject term describes.
4. Exclusive premises: because both premises are negative, no link is established between the subject and predicate terms.
5. Affirmative from a negative: the conclusion attempts to draw an affirmative conclusion from a negative premise.

In sentential logic

Fallacy of affirming the consequent:

1. If P, then Q.
2. Q.

   _____

3. Therefore, P.

Fallacy of denying the antecedent:

1. If P, then Q.
2. Not-P.

   _____

3. Therefore, Not-Q.

Informal fallacies

Fallacies of relevance

Ad populum: the fallacy of claiming that popularity establishes truth

Ad ignorantiam: the fallacy of supposing lack of proof proves something

Ad verecundiam: the fallacy of relying on an inappropriate authority

Red herring: the fallacy of changing the subject

    Ad baculum: appealing to force or threats

    Ad misericordiam: appealing to pity or guilt

Ad hominem: the fallacy of attacking the person instead of the argument

    Abusive: insulting or belittling the opponent

    Circumstantial: claiming the opponent is biased due to his circumstances

    Poisoning the well: connecting the opponent to something undesirable

    Tu quoque: accusing the opponent of hypocrisy

Fallacies of presumption

Hasty generalization: the fallacy of inferring from some to all

Begging the question: the fallacy of circular reasoning

False dilemma: the fallacy of reducing a variety of options to just two

Post hoc (false cause): The fallacy of assuming that x caused y simply because x preceded y

Straw man: the fallacy of oversimplifying the opponent's view to make it easy to refute

Fallacies of ambiguity

Is-ought: the fallacy of inferring a prescriptive statement from a descriptive statement

Amphiboly: the fallacy of creating two meanings through faulty sentence structure

Distribution: the fallacies of inferring from the whole to a part (division) and from a part to the whole (composition)

Equivocation: the fallacy of using the same word in two different ways

Index